D0333608

PHANTOMS
OF THE
RAILWAYS

W. B. HERBERT

DAVID & CHARLES
Newton Abbot   London   North Pomfret (Vt)

TO MY MOTHER

British Library Cataloguing in Publication Data
Herbert, W.B.
  Phantoms of the Railways
  1. Railways. Ghosts, to 1988
  I. Title
  133.1'22

ISBN 0-7153-9184-4

©W. B. Herbert 1988

All rights reserved. No part of this
publication may be reproduced, stored
in a retrieval system, or transmitted,
in any form or by any means, electronic
mechanical, photocopying, recording or
otherwise, without the prior permission
of David & Charles Publishers plc

Typeset by Typesetters (Birmingham) Limited,
Smethwick, Warley, West Midlands
and printed in Great Britain
by Billing & Sons Limited, Worcester
for David & Charles Publishers plc
Brunel House, Newton Abbot, Devon

Published in the United States of America
by David & Charles Inc
North Pomfret, Vermont 05053 USA

CONTENTS

FOREWORD

The publication of Barry Herbert's first volume of railway ghost stories seems to have awakened further restless spirits of a railway nature. Lurking in old engine sheds and tunnels, deserted station buildings and wayside halts the length and breadth of the kingdom, they have finally succumbed to the pen of the intrepid Mr Herbert.

Mr Herbert and I collaborated on what was a first published book for both of us. It concerned a long-closed Lincolnshire branch line which ran between Louth and Bardney. We explored the length of the line; even in broad daylight there was an overwhelming sense of the enduring presence of the railway at work, even though the line had closed many years previously. Those who profess not to believe in ghosts should visit such places.

Research, hard as it is, does, however, have its lighter moments. Conscientious as ever, Barry Herbert wrote to every preserved railway in the country asking for such stories (one concerning the Nene Valley is included in this volume). The opening line of one reply encouraged excited anticipation: 'Ghosts, we have hundreds of them', but elation was quickly dispelled by the next line: 'we call them members; they soon disappear when there is work to be done'.

If you have enjoyed the first volume of *Railway Ghosts* I commend this book for your further enjoyment.

A. J. LUDLAM
July 1988

1
THE PLATELAYERS' HUT

During my researches for material to complete this book I have found that railwaymen in particular have been reluctant to allow their names to be used in a story, and have sometimes insisted that even the name of the location be changed; perhaps they fear leg pulling from their workmates!

The following tale was recalled by a retired plate-layer ganger who, as expected, has asked me to change his name for the purpose of this story. He was certainly helpful but did also request that the name of the location be altered too. 'It's between Louth and Willoughby but I'm not saying exactly or we'll have the whole world knowing!' And he would not be drawn any further, so now read on.

I was told of the story by a friend who knew the old platelayer who we shall call Fred. My friend Harry (a retired driver) fixed up a meeting at a local pub and we were able to talk and discuss the strange happenings.

Fred's story concerned a lineside hut used by the permanent way men otherwise known as platelayers and/or lengthmen. The hut was situated in a cutting on the track-bed of the old East Lincolnshire line that ran between Grimsby and Peterborough via Boston; we are talking about the southern section of this once busy line.

What was so special about an old sleeper-built hut used by men to keep their tools and equipment in one side and take shelter from the elements in the other?

The local children used to play in the cutting and had for a long time fancied the hut as a den or HQ for their games, but the hut was always locked by a large padlock securing a hasp that was red with rust but still secured the door. Some of the more irresponsible youths had tried to set fire to the building but somehow it did not catch and went out much to their disappointment! The windows had been broken years ago but the railway company had boarded the frames up with wooden battens which were very effective; they did however allow a view into the building and although the children could see in they were fascinated with the place and were happy playing in the cutting.

All was uneventful until one child came home and told his mother that he had met a 'funny old man' in the cutting, 'dressed in funny old clothes'. The child was emphatic, 'but he just went away, we looked for him but couldn't find him'. His mother reassured him, 'people often go down there with their dogs; don't worry, I'm sure he wouldn't hurt you, but perhaps you shouldn't go down there for a week or two, David.'

A few weeks later and quite unrelated to David's experience a group of children from a neighbouring village made their way over the fields for a walk with their dogs. They found the cutting and scrambled down the slopes of the cutting enjoying the freedom, the old hut looked interesting and they soon explored the area, that had reverted back to nature. The flora and fauna had restablished its claim to colonise the old trackbed.

The children found the hut door opened easily enough and cautiously they ventured in, the place smelt musty and stale but it fascinated them. The remains of a table and chair told of more ordered times, spiders were everywhere, a mouse scuttled across the dirt floor startling the younger children who squeaked with fear. Chattering excitedly the children tried to open the other part of the building but it was still padlocked securely, they could see a little through various cracks but there seemed to be nothing of interest in that part.

One more adventurous boy decided to explore the overgrown slope behind the hut and he was pushing his way through the undergrowth when he caught sight of a figure approaching the hut further down the slope; the boy was close enough to see that the figure was that of a tramp wearing tattered clothing and crowned with a battered trilby hat. When the figure looked up the boy was impressed by bright, blue eyes and a long nose but a kind expression. Taken by surprise and fear of the other the boy lost his balance and tumbled down the grassy bank towards the stranger but to the boy's incredulous gaze the figure melted into thin air.

The other children hearing the boy's cries ran to him and he told them what had happened, they searched the cutting and the area around the hut without success. The other children pulled his leg and generally teased him about what he had seen but the child strenuously defended his story; somehow the fun had gone out of the adventure and they decided to return home.

The other boy, David, was also puzzling about his experience in the cutting and had resolved to go back and try to find out if he had been dreaming; somehow he did not feel frightened but more determined to see the tramp and make friends with him. One night when his parents were out David returned to the scene; as expected everything was quiet not even a walker with a dog was passing through, David cautiously approached the old hut, he peered through a crack in the battens before going round to the door which to his surprise was ajar. Very slowly he entered the hut, there was no one there, no sign of life only cobwebs and neglect. As he turned he caught a glimpse of something go past the open door, he dashed outside in time to see the figure of the old tramp going towards the slope as if to climb up and away. David ran after the figure that was nearly at the top, almost over the lip of the cutting, the figure then looked round to face the boy and smiled, then to David's amazement disappeared into thin air.

The boy searched around the area but the man, or

whatever had been a human, had gone leaving the boy bewildered and confused.

When he arrived home his parents had returned home and he was able to tell them what had happened; their first reaction was one of anger at his disregard of their wishes but they were interested in his story. Afterwards the boy's father decided to consult the local policeman to ask his views about the affair.

A day or two later the policeman called and was told about the strange experiences. 'I think I remember a tale long ago about a similar matter,' he said. He rubbed his chin, 'Some years ago a platelayer named Jed Knighton opted out of the rat race and became what I suppose you'd call a tramp. He wandered about this neck of the woods and he was quite harmless, he was fond of children. Anyway he lived in the old hut after the railway was taken up, we didn't see much of him in the winter but when the spring came round he would appear again. Then one year, about, well I can't remember when, we missed him. Some of us worried and went looking for him, then one of Alf Wood's sons found him dead in the old pw hut, we think he died of a heart attack or so the doctor said. Not a mark on him so it must have been natural causes; anyway it would seem that he comes back to his old home or sort of stamping ground. I'd heard tales about some people having seen an old man down there but not for a long while, he wouldn't hurt anyone so your lad needn't be scared of him.'

Fred says that was the last sighting of the spirit of Jed Knighton so his soul found its peace at last.

2
A STRANGE EXPERIENCE
AT WALTON JUNCTION

It was during the summer months of 1968 that my father first began taking me to Walton Junction, Liverpool to see what must have been the very last of the steam trains thunder past at 7 o'clock.

I loved trains, but I could remember the mounting excitement that I felt, as we approached the path leading to the station, change suddenly and inexplicably to fear.

The path ran parallel to the lines and junction box northwards towards the station itself. The fear always came when I was about halfway down the path. There was a strange feel about the place as though somebody or something was watching. It always seemed to mar our visits. The eyes even seemed to watch me when, during the autumn, I often picked wild blackberries at the end of the platform.

One particular Easter, a beautiful day, I remember an overwhelming fear filling me with absolute terror as we stood outside the ticket office after returning from a journey. It was indescribable and I intensely disliked that spot ever since.

During the damp November evenings when the gas lamp flickered in the wind, nothing would convince me that danger wasn't lurking in the eerie shadows.

During the summer of 1975 I visited the station one day when we had nothing particular to do, with two friends. I was astonished when we began walking down the now weed-strewn path to feel a familiar feeling of fear and expectation.

Both my friends felt that there was something 'queer'

about the place and we left quickly. A few weeks later we returned, this time with a third friend, a very level-headed girl. We told her nothing of our horrible experience. This time we settled in the deserted waiting room which was silent and cold.

After a very short time we all felt a horrible feeling of being watched and an intangible atmosphere of dread and doom. My third friend was very scared and wanted to go at once, feeling that we were in definite danger from something. We left as darkness was descending on that foreboding place and nothing could have made us stay or convinced us that there was not something awful waiting in the station.

Recently, I returned to Walton Junction with my children to get the train to Ormskirk. We used the same old path, and I was amazed to realise that without knowing it I had been hurrying my children along and constantly looking over my shoulder. I was convinced something was following us, though nothing was visible.

We paused on the small bridge which led to the ticket office, I looked at the now derelict railway cottages which stood silent, lost and forlorn. The feeling of fear had subsided somewhat and I remembered looking into the rubble-strewn backyards and thinking how sad it was that they were now in ruin, as last time I was at the station they were occupied. Suddenly, we all heard a loud bang from the back bedroom of the second cottage, as though a door had been slammed hard. It was a cold calm day with no wind.

We waited to see if anyone came out, maybe a cat or a dog, but everywhere was silent and still. There was so much rubbish and broken glass littered about anyway that it would have been difficult for anyone to climb out without making a lot of noise.

So we left and resumed our journey. The uncanny, oppressive atmosphere still hangs over that spot as it has done for over twenty years.

3

THE ISLE OF MAN,
THE RAMSEY MYSTERY

This story involves a youth hostel in the town of Ramsey in the Isle of Man whose narrow-gauge railway has brought pleasure and fascination to many people either as holiday makers or railway enthusiasts since the 1870s.

Let Mr J. Glasscock tell the story.

I can be reasonably precise about the date and time of the occurrence, it was at the Ramsey hostel and the time was 11.30pm in late July 1967 and I think it was a Wednesday.

1967 was the year that the Isle of Man Railway re-opened and I was feeling very emotional about the whole affair, with good reason, as the idea of the Isle of Man without a railway was quite unthinkable. I did actually get over to work for them in 1968–70 and 1971, but this story I am referring to was in 1967 when I was just paying a visit and was given a bed for the night in the hostel. There are two things to note about Ramsey Station; first of all, its extension line, the harbour branch, had closed years before, and secondly, no engine was ever kept at the station overnight because the shed water supply had been disconnected.

So I, and the only other lad in the dormitory, who was also a railway enthusiast, were surprised and stunned to hear, just as we were slipping off to sleep, the sound of wagons being shunted in the station. These wagons had a different coupling system over in the island; the sound of I O M shunting is quite different from mainland shunting, you don't get the clunk of the links on a loose-coupled wagon but a delayed clank as the 'chopper' of one drops over the buffing plate of another. When you have listened to it many times as we had, you get to recognise the unique sound, it is absolutely unmistakable.

At first, we could only hear the wagons and we thought that it could be someone hand-shunting, but at this time of night? Also we couldn't understand why, since there were only three trains a day each way, and only the 11.50am arrival and the 4.05pm departure were ever heavy trains. We only knew for certain that there was something strange afoot when we heard the sounds of a train being marshalled and it started coming towards the hostel, what is more terrifying was that it was coming on a non-existent track! Had it been a real train the sound would have faded off towards the west – away from the hostel. Instead – and we could now hear the engine as well – it came towards the hostel over the non-existent harbour branch and clattered to a stop, perhaps at one of the wharves. And then we heard one final hiss of the safety valves and then silence.

There were seven people in our dormitory and I think five were awake; we all heard the mysterious sounds without any doubt but it appeared that none of the inhabitants of the other dormitories heard anything at all. We, of course, went outside to see if we could see anything, not really expecting to; there was nothing to suggest the passage of a train, just the cool night air and the distant sound of night life, nothing to prove or disprove the eerie sounds we had heard so clearly. Was it wishful thinking? Could I have been dreaming? I think not as four other unsolicited accounts verified my experience. We had been privy to a re-enactment of the movements of a former working on the old harbour branch, and although not frightened we were all very puzzled by the strange sequence of events.

4

ASHTON MOSS JUNCTION

There would appear to be a considerable number of strange events concerning signal boxes and their environs more so than other areas of unexplained activities. In spite of many attempts to allay fears and promotion of the normal working conditions by the railway authorities, signal boxes are rather emotive places and one doesn't have to have a very fertile imagination to get into the feeling of unease and expectancy.

However, a story, again entirely without explanation, concerns Ashton Moss Junction, but let Mr Ian McGill reveal the mystery.

This story concerns a location about $^3/_4$ mile west of Ashton-under-Lyme Station where a freight-only line from Denton Junction on the Stockport to Stalybridge line bifurcates to join the Manchester to Huddersfield Trans Pennine route by way of west and east facing curves. The point of bifurcation at the southernmost point of the triangle is Ashton Moss South Junction, whilst the western and eastern points of convergence with the Manchester to Huddersfield line are known as Ashton Moss North Junction and OA & GB (Oldham Ashton & Guide Bridge Junctions) respectively.

My informant (who wishes to be anonymous but nevertheless truthful) had spent a short time in his early days as a signalman at OA & GB Junction signal box. Whilst on duty one Saturday afternoon during the early part of 1975, he heard the sound of footsteps ascending the steps leading up to the box, then he became aware of the figure of a man about to enter the lobby or vestibule outside the door. Expecting the visitor to knock to gain admittance, the signalman walked towards the door to see what the visitor wanted. However, the anticipated knock never came and opening the door of the box he found the lobby silent and totally devoid of anyone, the strange visitor had vanished without trace. The signalman went down the steps to search for signs of the visitor but there was no one about. A complete mystery.

The brief glimpse the signalman gained of the stranger was not sufficient to give a good description except that he was male and he appeared to be carrying a bag. Was this the shade of a railwayman visiting his former workplace? Could he have been a signalman who met an unfortunate death and still haunts the place of his end? To continue:

The following Saturday afternoon, my informant was once again on duty when the light began to fade – he hated the short winter days; suddenly he heard a sound, a strange sound of movement below the box. He went to the top of the steps and looked around, he couldn't see anyone or anything untoward; he looked out of the window and he thought he saw a figure on or around the track. In the vicinity of a road bridge, which spanned the line near Ashton Moss South Junction, about 200 yards away to the south, the signalman at Ashton Moss North Junction box also became aware of someone out on the track whom he took to be trespassing. After conferring, the two signalmen decided to try and apprehend the person concerned, and after making sure that the control had been told of the situation and the boxes were safe to leave they walked towards each other, approaching the trespasser from opposite directions, so keeping him in view all the time and affording him little chance of escape. Nevertheless, on reaching the spot where they had seen a person loitering, there was no one to be seen.

I don't have to stress the danger of anyone moving about on a railway track; ignorance is no excuse for trespassing on railway property and the warning notices are always abundant, which is the reason that the two men were so concerned, firstly for the person's safety and secondly for the risk of a collision with a train and the undoubted injuries that would result. The two men were not concerned with ghosts, only the safe operation of the signal box and its environs.

The person they sought had disappeared into thin air; it was only then did they puzzle and wonder if the dusk had conned them into imagining that they could be mistaken. I could understand one man imagining that he saw a person in the immediate area of the box but it is hard to believe that two level-headed signalmen could have been mistaken enough to be confused by the same phenomenon. My informant thinks that what he saw was genuine and was certain that someone was down there, his mate in the other box was equally sure that he too saw the figure. If any person had the authority to be in the vicinity he would be wearing a high visibility vest, as laid down in the Railway Regulations, it would be madness not to do so.

I am told that other people have had similar experiences but are not prepared to enlarge on their stories; perhaps they had seen a ghost of a long-gone railwayman who had worked in the area years ago and had come back to his earthly place of employment! The mystery remains and perhaps will never be solved, but one thing is for sure, those two signalmen were absolutely certain of what they had seen and were unshakeable in their beliefs.

5

LYONSHALL STATION

The village of Lyonshall in Herefordshire near the Welsh borders was provided with a station by the Great Western Railway; this station had a somewhat chequered history and a rather inconsistent patronage.

The small railway outpost had the Indian sign on it when closure came entirely on 1 January 1917 in the midst of World War I. However, some five years later the GWR had a change of heart and decided to reopen the station to goods traffic on 18 September 1922. Subsequent re-opening to passengers on 11 December 1922 heralded a new era for the station and trade seemed to have awakened to the transport needs of the community.

But again in a wartime emergency, when one would imagine that *all* railway stations would be needed during a war, the axe fell again on Lyonshall Station and it was closed to all traffic on 1 July 1940 and abandoned.

My correspondent, Mr Glasscock of Braintree, Essex, has a very strange tale to tell that even today has no logical explanation.

During the hot summer of 1959, on a particularly heavy and sultry day and following morning, I and a friend visited Lyonshall Station. We were on a cycling holiday and me being very interested in railways generally, liked looking over old stations.

Lyonshall Station was, and I very much doubt that any trace of it remains today, in a very dangerous condition. The bridge had been removed but the wooden platform and building were visible from the road below; there was a roofed stairway leading to platform level, every step was either missing or rotten, so the bottom of the staircase was made completely inaccessible with barbed wire criss-crossed right up to the old roof beam. Over the years brambles had spread in all directions and had wound round the barbed wire, so it would have taken an axe or some other sharp tool to have gained entry, one certainly couldn't have reached the top of the stairway at all.

The general condition was extremely dangerous and one could expect difficulty in trying to gain any access as the stairway was so derelict.

I remarked to my friend, 'You'd have to wait for a long time to get a train from here,' he smiled and we both set off for the youth hostel down the road. I believe that it is closed now.

In the morning, though our route lay the other way, I insisted on going back to the old station for one more look. It seemed sad to see the old place decaying, uncared for and neglected. I was convinced that something had happened in our absence; something had indeed happened – it had rained hard during the night and early morning – which was strange for that summer when we had a period of almost drought conditions. Anyway the steps that remained, and there weren't many of them, were still damp since the roof of the stairway was as rotten as everything else. But so clearly visible and definitely new since the previous evening was a set of footprints, and looking around, a set of tracks, small hob-nailed boot tracks going up the staircase to the top and not coming down. I shuddered, the very thought of anyone being so foolish baffled me, the steps were so rotten that it wouldn't have taken any weight to have snapped them and sent anyone plunging down causing a bad injury.

The prints were about my own size, $6^1/_2$ and my own guess for what it is worth, since, as a cadet I did own a pair of hob-nails, is that my own almost religious love of country railways had revealed a kind of secular stigmatic effect. My friend was most unimpressed, he had seen the footprints but shrugged his shoulders and suggested that we move on. However, the mystery remains and I will never forget it and will always puzzle over the mysterious footprints that defied all the obstacles, or did they?

6

THE SCENT OF THE ROSE

Charlotte Campbell was more than delighted to have received a reply to her letter for the position of children's nanny which she had seen advertised in *The Times*. She hoped for a reply, but dared not hope too much; she imagined that the Hon Mrs Anderson-Hunt would have had many replies and perhaps ladies with experience would be far more preferable to a young comparatively inexperienced girl like her. But in 1906 it was the accepted procedure to reply to letters and Charlotte was so excited at the invitation to visit Winstable Hall for an interview.

The Hon Mrs Anderson-Hunt had sent a crisp 10s note for her train fare and expenses, and that sum would adequately cover those. Charlotte couldn't contain her delight.

Never having been more than ten miles from her parents' home in her nineteen years the prospect of a fifty-mile train journey seemed like an adventure and she would travel alone, but maybe she would meet some handsome young man! She smiled at the thought; the next seven days to the interview seemed almost endless in the long hot summer of 1906.

Charlotte woke very early on 21 September, giving herself plenty of time to make the very best of herself, putting on her Sunday best dress and bonnet. Her heart was beating much faster as she approached the railway station, she offered her 10s note to the booking clerk and received her return ticket to Wiltham which was the nearest station to Winstable Hall. There according to her letter a trap would be waiting to convey her to the Hall.

Charlotte walked slowly onto the platform and waited for her train to pull in. Soon a plume of smoke heralded its arrival and Charlotte was held in awe as the gleaming locomotive hauled the immaculate rake of teak coaches into the station. The engine stopped alongside her and a young man with blond hair and a cheery smile jumped down. 'Hello,' he greeted. She smiled demurely. 'How far are you going?' Charlotte replied that she was going to Wiltham and she had an important interview. The young man said he would tell her when to get off and then busied himself with an oilcan among the driving wheels.

Charlotte stepped into the first compartment and sat down, the station was now a hive of activity; Charlotte leaned out of the window and watched the guard's van being loaded up with milk churns, sacks of mail, and boxes of red roses. The other passengers had found their seats, the whistle blew, and the young fireman leaned over the door and handed Charlotte a single red rose. Smiling, Charlotte thanked him. 'I'm Albert,' he smiled.

It was not a long journey and as the sun was shining it was a very pleasant one. Eventually the train pulled into Wiltham and Albert leapt down and opened the carriage door, taking Charlotte's hand and helping her down. 'There we are, I hope you get the post!' Charlotte thanked him and passed through the barrier into the station yard where a uniformed coachman was waiting with a trim little gig to take her to meet the Hon Mrs Anderson-Hunt.

Charlotte did get the position of nanny and often travelled on the same train home on her days off, always in the first compartment behind the tender and always hoping that she would see Albert, which she often did and she leaned out of the window to talk to him when the train stopped in the stations.

It was over a year before Charlotte was allowed to take her charge, a little boy called Edward, home with her to meet her family on her day off. It was a very sunny day and it was made all the more complete by Albert being on duty on the return journey. He had jumped down to open the carriage door for her and Charlotte and the child made to get in. Albert was talking to them as they waited to leave, and the boy had a large rubber ball that he would insist on throwing about in the compartment. Charlotte, her eyes on Albert who was taking her attention, asked him rather half-heartedly to desist, but the boy threw the ball out of the window. It hit the platform fence and ran under the carriage; as quick as a flash the boy darted past Charlotte and Albert and tried to look for it under the wheels. As Charlotte scrambled out of the carriage the boy was halfway under the carriage; almost beside herself, Charlotte and Albert tried to haul him up. The driver had seen the green flag and had opened the regulator to ease forward, yelling at Albert to come on. By this time Charlotte was halfway under the carriage with Albert trying to help her. The boy had got jammed and couldn't get out. The train eased forward, the driver unaware of the panic. Charlotte screamed, the driver panicked, his hand still on the regulator. Albert leapt onto the footplate, missed his footing and grabbed the regulator to stop himself falling; the train moved forward dragging the nanny and child under the wheels. Nothing could save them, the wheels had passed over them and life had gone.

But that was not the end of this sad story, nor of the nanny and child who died so horribly.

Many people have seen Charlotte waiting for Albert, or her ghost who refuses to leave this station. Albert was so distressed by the whole affair that he applied for another post further away from the scene of the tragedy.

But sightings of the young lady continued and the curious point was that people used to say that in the first compartment next to the tender there would often be the strong scent of roses.

After a while the station returned to normal, Charlotte hadn't been seen for some time, and Albert had been killed in World War I so all three participants in the awful tragedy had gone for ever, or had they?

Just before the outbreak of World War II a long passenger train was in the station taking water. The driver was oiling an axle box when he turned round to see the trim figure of a young lady with a small boy near the first compartment of the carriage next to the tender. He made as if to talk to them when they melted before his very eyes; he couldn't believe it and as the guard approached he told him what he had seen. The guard smiled, 'It's Charlotte and the boy, we've seen her on many occasions. By the way, can you smell that lovely scent of roses?'

7

THE FURNESS RAILWAY MYSTERY

I am very grateful to Mr R. R. Mester for the following story of strange happenings on a long abandoned stretch of railway between Goldmire Junction and Millwood Junction on the original line of the Furness Railway.

My correspondent's earliest and most vivid recollection of a haunted railway line dates from childhood memories of some sixty years ago and refers to the short length of line between Goldmire Junction and Millwood Junction on the old Furness Railway in the area of Dalton-in-Furness.

Opened in 1846 this section had been early superseded and closed and in the time of Mr Mester's childhood comprised only an overgrown formation. There were many trees and shrubs about so visibility was rather restricted, a footpath crossed both railway and stream just below Millwood, and there was a large detached residence. It was a creepy spot with a strong pungent smell of garlic and there was always a feeling of tension and foreboding.

Frequently and for no apparent reason, there would be a chilling burst of wind and a roar as of a passing train. In the gloaming it was possible to glimpse passing lights identical to those of a carriage in a moving train, altogether it was an eerie happening – crossing a long-abandoned railway in the Vale of Nightshade!

Down in the Vale lay the ruins of Furness Abbey – founded by one king (Stephen) and destroyed by another king, Henry VIII, at the Dissolution of the Monasteries. The roar was held by some to be that of the dispossessed and not a train at all. My fears were shared by youthful friends and even adult relatives at times seemed to 'chivvy' us along as if they too expected the ghost train to rush by. Some seemed quite certain of a mystery train – one they heard that came and vanished but was never recognised.

Years later it seemed reasonable to identify the ghost train with nearby trains on well concealed tracks linking Dalton-in-Furness with Askam-in-Furness and Barrow-in-Furness respectively, but this explanation did not entirely remove the doubts and fears experienced even in retrospect.

Maybe there was a mystery train of sorts deriving from some forgotten tale in an area served early by rail linking with wild and remote sea shores. Whatever the explanation, for some of us there was always a sense of fear in this secluded spot and that moreover linked to a train.

Perhaps it was no more than old *Coppernob*, Furness Railway No 3, built in 1846 and resident in those school days in its great glass case outside Barrow Central Station, taking a turn over its old hunting grounds . . .

8

THE SPIRIT ENTITY

I have called this story the Spirit Entity because it illustrates the fact that earthbound factions are still very active, and making their presence felt in so many unexpected ways. I am indebted to my correspondent Mrs D. M. Ross for this compelling tale.

Mrs Ross was one of six senior citizens travelling between Glasgow and Paisley in a DMU; they were in the rear carriage with the brake unit in the centre. The train braked to a shuddering halt at the Paisley signal box where it remained for the next thirty minutes whilst the driver and guard proceeded to examine the underside and topside of the train. Eventually the guard climbed aboard and entered Mrs Ross's carriage and demanded to know who had pulled the communication cord which none of the passengers could see from their seated position. When the guard was told that no one had moved from their seats he became very worried because he said he had to make out a report to British Rail as to the cause of the delay and he then said, 'I'll have to put it down to person or persons unknown'. To which one lady said, 'That would be a complete lie, have you never heard of a Spirit Entity?'

The central position of the brake section prevented anyone moving along the train without being noticed, the guard agreed to this point. It did not solve his problem but the poor fellow had to make out his report and he had to find some element of evidence and so far he hadn't got much to write down. How the poor fellow finally got his report together I do not know but I doubt that even he didn't realise that he was

27

dealing with a supernatural force that did what it liked when it liked.

Mrs Ross tells me that she later discovered that several years earlier near Paisley signal box two trains had collided with loss of life. My informant tells me that she feels sure that the earlier event is still 'earthbound' and repeated the action. I imagine that the frustrated passengers would not be amused if they realised that the delay was caused by a restless spirit but the report of the accident can be checked in British Rail's archives.

So this strange occasion and its tragic precedent can be the work of the past or present spirit entity . . .

9
YARWELL TUNNEL

I am very grateful to Mr H. E. Caunt, the Public Relations Officer for the Nene Valley Railway in Cambridgeshire, who kindly sent me details of the strange happenings concerning Yarwell Tunnel.

During the construction of the Blisworth to Peterborough branch line of the old London & Birmingham Railway in 1845, the engineer and surveyor of the route, one Robert Stephenson, being faced with a hilly terrain near to the villages of Yarwell and Wansford decided to tunnel through as a cutting was not practicable at that time.

Hence gangs of navvies (mainly Irish) were set to work on the task of excavation and works; they lived in mud huts, huts which would only offer the most primitive shelter from the elements. Kilns were established to manufacture the bricks used to line the tunnel (approximately one million were made), and the clay used came by barges on the nearby Nene. Weekends were a particularly troublesome time, drunkenness and fighting was a real problem and special police had to be drafted in to take charge. It was reported at the time that ten or more navvies met their death fighting and falling from scaffolding as this tunnel is unusually high and was built to accommodate double tracks.

The late Mr Walter Gilbey used to tell of many strange happenings during maintenance work in the tunnel; mysterious noises, agonising cries and sounds of men fighting. Hammers and shovels used to disappear without trace, a newly laid stretch of track was found the following morning with all the wooden keys on the tunnel side all knocked out. Sabotage was suspected but after a thorough investigation was never proved.

On another occasion some gangers had to jump for their lives as a freight train suddenly entered the tunnel without any warning from the lookout men at either end of the tunnel. As soon as the train had cleared the tunnel the gangers found one of the lookout men lying unconscious by the side of the track. On reviving him the man told the head ganger that he had been struck by a blow at the back of the head yet medical evidence revealed no sign of injury, furthermore his whistle, flags, and lamp were never found.

Another strange happening concerns a one-time station master at Wansford Station who had a pet cat called Snowy which used to follow him everywhere. One late autumn afternoon Snowy failed to turn up for his meal, so his master went out to look for him. Unfortunately the station master was rather deaf and he failed to hear an approaching train in the inky darkness of the tunnel and he was struck down and killed. Snowy was never seen again.

Yet on many occasions a greyish-white cat has been seen crying piteously entering the tunnel never to reappear; none of the local cats are like Snowy, being either black, black-and-white, ginger or tortoiseshell!

So Yarwell Tunnel has its mysterious and macabre secrets, sharing with some these facets and leaving an indelible memory in the mind.

10

BRIDGE 173

Bridge 173 was an agricultural occupation bridge spanning a deep railway cutting and was used by the local farmer to give access to both big lineside fields.

It was a very sound brick structure and had been built about 1868 but it had the notorious reputation of being called 'Lover's Leap', no doubt due to the fact that several suicide attempts had been made from its high parapet, most of them fatal.

One particular night, young John Armitage, a very junior passed engine cleaner had no notion of the bridge's notoriety. He had just fired up and sat down to rest. His mate, driver Sam Webster, gave him a smile of approval and said, 'Good lad, young John, now put your injector on, shut it off when you've got nearly a full "glass", then have a few minutes. I'll tell you when to fire up again just before we go up the bank.' Young John did as he was told. This was his first mainline trip and he was grateful to Sam for his advice and also for him taking him on this trip.

The shed running foreman had asked Sam if he would take young John as there was no one available at the time. He explained that although the lad had not been on the mainline before, he was a good, reliable and sensible lad. Sam, without any hesitation had agreed knowing that to wait for the first available fireman would delay his train's departure. Young John had been delighted. He had done a reasonable amount of pilot work, firing for some of the older shunt link drivers and had also fired on the local 'pick-up', but this at last was the real thing.

So far, driver Sam Webster was pleased with his young

mate's performance and had noted with approval how he used his firing shovel to spread the coal systematically round the firebox and his ability to fire up through the firehole door trap without having to open the door. With a little bit more experience and confidence, he would un-doubtedly make a 'good 'un'.

Young John, seated on his cabside fireman's seat, looked interestedly about him. Poking his head out from the cab, to get a little cooling draught, he noticed that they were about to enter a long deep cutting and marvelled at the way the cutting must have been cut through al-most solid rock. The track took a right hand curve and for the first time he saw the bridge standing high above the track. Approaching the bridge, he had a shock. Al-though it was getting dusk, he was certain that he had seen someone or something fall from the bridge.

Frozen with shock, momentarily, he recovered his scattered wits and shouted, 'Sam, stop; someone's jumped off the bridge.' Sam acted quickly. As a mainline driver, his reflexes were excellent. Smartly closing the regula-tor, he made a partial application of the steam brake, paused, released it, paused once again, then when he heard the wagon buffers face up, he made a full brake application. He knew of course that he would never be able to halt the train before it reached the bridge and he had his guard's safety to think about. If he had made a full brake application, his guard, Gerry Briggs, would have been thrown from one end of the brakevan to the other with a possible resultant injury.

As the train slowed down, Sam came over to the fireman's side and looked out and seeing nothing, sud-denly realised the legend of the bridge. He looked at young John, now white and shaken with the shock. 'Don't worry, young John,' he said, to comfort and reassure him. 'You kept a good lookout.' As the train slowed to a halt, he remembered other drivers, mostly some of the 'old hands', talk about Bridge 173 and

how some of them joked about the 'strange sightings'
near it.

With the train stopping about a train's length beyond
the bridge, he knew that he would have to walk back and
explain to Gerry and have a look. 'Stop on the engine,
John,' he said. 'I'll go back and have a look and see the
guard.' Walking back to the end of the train, he found
the guard standing on the track beside his brakevan.
'What's up then, Sam?' he asked. 'Anything wrong with
the engine?' 'No,' Sam said. 'My mate thought he saw
something or someone fall off the bridge.'

The guard climbed up into his brakevan, to return
with a can of detonators in case he had to protect the
train. 'Come on then, Sam, let's have a look.' Reaching
the bridge, they had a good look round but found nothing.
'Bloody bridge,' Gerry said, 'the last time this happened was
about five years ago, when Jack Thompson saw something.
Do you remember everybody laughed about it? Come on,
Sam, let's get going. If we get a move on, we'll make the
time up. I don't think we should report it, do you?' 'Not
so likely,' Sam agreed. 'I'll tell young John not to say
anything.' Quickly they returned to the train and once
more started off. On the move once again, Sam told his
young fireman all about the legend of the bridge. 'Will
you have to report it?' John asked. 'Not so bloody likely,'
Sam said. 'If I tell anyone that we stopped to look for a
ghost, they'll laugh at me, and if I was you, I wouldn't
tell your mates either. Just tell them that you know now
where Bridge 173 is.'

11

THE BARMAN'S STORY –
A SEQUEL TO BRIDGE 173

It was a sunny autumn afternoon in 1963 as John and Mary Briggs were walking along a disused trackbed in the Westcountry with their two Jack Russell terriers, Tina and Spot, who were enjoying their walk as much as their owners. There was so much to sniff at and they had already found two rabbits and had aroused a flock of partridges.

When they reached the approach to what appeared to be a long deep cutting, Mary stopped. 'Let's go back, I think we've gone far enough and it looks dark and spooky.' Was it a woman's intuition? The two dogs settled the matter, racing on ahead. John looked at his watch, 'Come on Mary, we can go on for another ten minutes and I'd like to find out what is around that bend.' So reluctantly she followed her husband through the cutting. Eventually they saw ahead of them the bridge standing high and spanning the valley; red crumbling brick it stood, carrying a farm road and seldom used by anyone else. As they drew nearer John could just make out a plate on which the number 173 was discernible.

Suddenly, the dogs who were sniffing this exciting new country stopped; ears raised, hair rising on their necks, they backed slowly towards John and Mary, then they howled and turned and ran back through the cutting, leaving John and Mary puzzled and a bit frightened. Mary shuddered 'I don't like this place, it seems sad and depressing, don't you think it's turned cold?' John had to agree, he too felt a bit uneasy and scared but didn't want to show his fear to Mary. 'OK, let's go back to the hotel, then we'll have a nice cup of tea.' Mary smiled and kissed him.

Later that evening when they were seated comfortably in the bar Mary brought up the subject of the eerie feeling in the cutting; they agreed it had been a most disturbing experience and that there must be some explanation. John said 'I'll ask the barman if he knows anything about it.' Steve, the barman, was polishing a glass as John approached the bar. 'Now sir, what can I get you?' he asked. John ordered a pint of bitter and a sweet martini. While Steve was busying himself John asked him about the bridge and the strange feeling in the cutting. Steve placed the drinks on the counter, 'There we are, sir, that will be . . .' After the till drawer closed, he turned and said, 'Bridge 173 sir? It's haunted, and I would keep well away from it. It's bad news around here sir, and the bridge seems to attract suicides. They used to come here, yes, to this hotel to spend their last nights before they went to that bridge to hurl themselves off, sometimes in front of a train; but now the line has gone and the track removed we don't get so many nuts coming to end their days. Now only Alf Hurst, he farms the land either side of the cutting, uses it to get across but even Alf doesn't like it. The wind always blows cold in that cutting and across the old bridge.'

John listened, fascinated with Steve's story. 'Mary and I took our dogs down there this afternoon and I must admit we didn't like it, Mary was quite frightened. We won't go again I can assure you.' Steve nodded, 'Very wise sir, they used to call the spot under the bridge, "Lover's Leap". It's a brooding, desolate place that.' Mary came over to the bar, on that the two men stopped talking and smiled at her. 'Can I have my drink, it seems as if you two will talk all night,' she said. 'Let's go and sit down, dear,' she said to her husband. She took his arm, 'Just a minute sir,' said Steve. Mary took her drink to her seat and prepared to wait again. 'One thing that might interest you, last year our manager jumped from that bridge and broke his neck . . .'

12

THE OLD LOCO SHED

The old loco shed stood gaunt, derelict and roofless, amidst the mounds of brick rubble and refuse surrounding it. The once busy shed, now with the skeletal, unclad girders of its roof standing stark against the darkening sky, was just a ghost of its former self. As it was soon to be finally and completely demolished, I took the first opportunity of looking round and about the old shed to see if I could find something, anything, of interest relating to the depot to add to my growing collection of 'Railwayana'.

The loco shed had many sentimental memories for me as my late father had been a mainline driver there many years ago before the branch line, with its four stations, marshalling sidings, loco shed and workshops closed, shortly after the closure of the two adjacent collieries. The branch line had survived for a few years as a single line until its final demise.

As I passed what had been the marshalling yard and sidings, I glanced at the rows of rusting buffer stops and rotting wooden buffer beams, and conjured up a picture of its lines of laden coal wagons waiting to be despatched and the coal empties waiting to be taken to the collieries to be filled. It was a cold, wet, typically late autumnal afternoon as I walked along the old trackbed, avoiding the many puddles of murky rainwater on my way. I stopped momentarily to look at the old 'cenotaph' or what remained of it. The once modern coaling plant was now just a mass of huge broken lumps of concrete. Would there be anything collectable there, I wondered. I decided against looking into the tumbledown wooden hut that had once housed the coal hopper controls. The rotting wooden walkway looked too perilous to risk any injury so I continued on my way to the shed, now some seventy or eighty yards away. I stopped about twenty yards away from the shed, appalled at the scene of utter desolation and neglect. One of the shed's huge, wooden doors, the only survivor, hung crazily, on one rusting hinge, swaying slightly in the stiffening breeze. Continuing on my way, I saw that the outer and inner ash pits were filled with rubble and rubbish of every kind. What an inglorious end to what had once been a busy loco shed that had been the scene of so much activity in its heyday. Reaching the shed, I stepped over several mounds of brick and other rubble and went inside, looking carefully at the wet streaked brick walls searching for anything that could be identifiable with the depot. One of the rusting iron pipes fastened to the shed wall and apparently coming from what remained of the old boilerhouse inside, had a plate affixed to it, near the stump of what must have been a water stop valve.

It could be of interest, so taking a piece of cotton waste out of my pocket, I cleaned the accumulated filth off it, only to discover that on it was stamped ON↔OFF. However, as it was brass, I decided that it was collectable. It was something at least. Taking the roll of tools out of my stout and well travelled haversack, I unscrewed the plate with only a little difficulty and put it into the haversack. I had got one souvenir and if not identifiable with the shed, at least I knew where it had come from. Walking further into the shed, I paused and looked around wondering how many times my old father must have walked through it. Then, on an impulse, I retraced my steps following the run of the old water washout pipes until I found myself in the remains of what must have been the old boilerhouse. It was there that I made my one and only good find, not of course taking into account the brass washout pipe plate. I saw a corner of what looked like a rusted iron plate protruding from a pile of brick rubble. Eagerly I set about to free it from its rubble prison. It took me about three or four minutes to rescue it and I looked at my 'prize'. Cleaning the muck off it I was delighted with my discovery. It read, 'LNWR–BOILERHOUSE–PRIVATE', and must have come off the boilerhouse door. It was not too big or cumbersome to take away so I packed it up in my stout old haversack and stepping out of the ruins of the boilerhouse, returned to the shed. It was getting dark and the wind had freshened, the rain gusting through the length of the shed so I decided that it was time to pack up and head for the nearest hospitable pub where I had been told I would be able to get a good meal of hot pie and peas. Dad had often spoken about the Railway Hotel just across the road from what remained of the station, and how he used to play the battered old piano and have a sing-song with his pals. Perhaps I would be able to conjure up his image while indulging myself with my pie and peas and a pint. On my way out of the shed, I suddenly realised that I was not on my own. There, walking down the middle of the shed in the gloom, I espied a dark blue-clad figure wearing what appeared to be what Dad used to call a 'steamraiser', a shiny topped peaked cap. The figure walked slowly down the shed. I was unable to see his face but as it was getting dark, I was not surprised. I was just about to speak when suddenly, abruptly, the figure disappeared. Had it been a figment of imagination, brought about with the increasing gloom, and the aura of the surrounding dereliction? No, I knew that I had seen someone, or something. I had never believed in ghosts but what I had seen was unaccountable. Suddenly, I heard a loud crash near me, scaring me out of my wits. The old shed door hanging on one rusted hinge, would swing no more and had crashed to the floor. It was enough for me, the last straw. I had seen and heard enough. Already startled by the apparition, the crashing down of the big heavy door completely unnerved me.

I ran out of the shed not looking back, raced across the old marshalling yard, out of the tumbledown gateway of the station, across the road and into the brightly lit warmth of the Railway Hotel bar. Faces looked strangely at me as I burst abruptly into the bar room. One old chap said, 'What's up lad, tha' looks as if tha's seen a ghost!' After getting my breath, I said, 'I think I have'. One kindly old chap stood up and said, 'Come on mate, sit down here, I'll get you a pint then you can tell us your story.' As I sat down, one old boy seated next to me said, 'Have you been walking on the old trackbed then?' 'Yes,' I replied. Another said, 'I bet you've been into the loco shed.' 'Yes,' I said. 'How did you know?' 'Tha's not first one to get a shock there mate,' he answered. 'What did you see then?' I then told them about the apparition, how I had seen someone walking down the shed and then suddenly disappearing. The kindly old chap who gave up his seat for me brought me my pint saying 'Drink this mate, you'll feel better when tha's supped that.' While I gratefully sipped my pint, they told me the story. Several people apart from myself had seen the 'loco apparition'. Between them, my new-found friends told me the story.

While the branch line and the loco shed was working, a driver from the shed had unfortunately failed the railway doctor with defective colour vision and as a result had been relegated to fire-lighting and steam-raising duties. He used to come in here regularly for a pint, they said. The chap who had been kind enough to get me my pint said, 'I was only a young chap at the time but I remember him well. Fred Grisenthwaite were his name. He were never the same when he came off mainline. It was a pity too about his accident as if he hadn't had enough bad luck.' 'What happened then?' I asked. 'He were firin' up and steamin' an engine when it happened. A tube burst and the blow back threw him back against the tender end. He must have hit his head for it killed him. At the time we said "poor old Fred, we'll never see him again." We haven't, but others have, including you now evidently.' I had by now recovered my scattered senses and after finishing off my enjoyable meal of pie and peas and my second pint, I thanked my kind new-found friends and left the hospitable Railway bar to walk back down to where my trusty old Morris Minor was parked. It had without doubt been a day to remember and now whenever I look at my LNWR Boilerhouse Private plate, I think of poor unfortunate Fred Grisenthwaite and his tragic demise, and then recall the Railway Hotel bar room and the kind friends I met that night.

13

GLASGOW UNDERGROUND HAUNTINGS!

The Glasgow underground railway system like the London underground counterpart has some very strange and totally unexplained events. The sceptics will scoff as usual but my informants are adamant in their accounts of the happenings.

The Glasgow system runs in a circle beneath the city centre and is narrow gauge 4ft; it serves a pressing transport need. It also plays host to a number of strange, ghostly occurrences according to a book *I belong to Glasgow* by Bill Hamilton and Gordon Carsely, from which I am most obliged for the information.

The aforementioned book was written before the system closed for extensive modernisation and I have no further information (in spite of research) that any more unexplained events have occurred.

In the old days there was no physical access from the running lines to Govan car sheds and workshops, so stock was only brought out of the tunnels for repair and maintenance, which necessitated lifting the vehicles bodily off the track and up through pits into the workshops by means of a large overhead crane. At night after close of the service it was the practice to stable the empty trains end to end on the running lines in the tunnels on each side of the shed car pits, the end doors of each vehicle opened to permit ready exit of passengers in the event of an emergency, and to allow access to the lines of stabled trains by cleaners and others whose nocturnal duties took them into the subway tunnels.

On one occasion a team of five men went down into the tunnels for which purpose they had to pass through the line of empty stabled cars. On reaching the last train they found a colleague talking to a middle-aged man dressed in a light-coloured rain coat and flat cap who was assumed to have been overcarried on the last train after going out of service at Capland Road Station. The stranger was led back through the empty trains to the car shed pits where he could gain access to the street. Looking back at regular intervals to see if the stranger was following, eventually they reached the access to the street but the guide was astonished to find the man had vanished into thin air. The men went back and searched the trains but the man had disappeared; all the men agreed the man had been there, they had all seen him, they were all completely baffled.

Govan car sheds were reputedly haunted by a figure which was seen from time to time in a driving compartment of a car but on investigation the figure had disappeared and was nowhere to be found; the cab was empty yet strangely cold! Cleaners working in the tunnels between Kelvinbridge and Hillhead Stations used to report hearing disembodied voices of women singing.

An accident in 1922 is believed to be the explanation for the appearance of the 'Grey Lady' whose ghostly form has been reported in the tunnel near Shields Road Station. In that year a lady and a little girl (presumably the daughter) fell from an otherwise deserted station platform into the path of an oncoming train; the station master on seeing the incident attempted to rescue them both but was only able to save the girl.

Two maintenance gangs who were working one night some distance apart on a section of track noticed a mysterious light between them but despite searching the area nothing could be found to explain the phenomenon. Finally, at around 3am one Sunday in 1967 pump man, Willie Baxter, was detailed to go through the tunnels from St Enochs to Bridge Street Station where he was to attend to a tank located beneath the stairs. After walking for some time, having covered about half the distance between the two stations, Willie became aware of a steady, yet rather unnerving sound just ahead as if someone was hammering the rails. The ganger, whose section this was and who might therefore have been responsible, had passed through some ninety minutes earlier. Willie Baxter was gripped by fear, he didn't understand it, he hated the dark tunnels, he stopped walking and the noise stopped; by now Willie was probably near the point where the tunnels passed under the River Clyde and it was said that it was possible to hear the sound of a ship's propeller whenever a vessel passed overhead. However, Willie was certain that this could not account for the strange noise, so he continued, only to find the noise started again even louder. That was it! He'd had enough, he turned and ran for his life back to St Enochs and the fresh air.

Later discussing the experience with his workmates the reaction was divided, some voiced complete disbelief, some agreed as they too had had similar experiences, others just nodded agreement with Willie. I am told that there have been further incidents since the system reopened but so far nobody has come along with any details.

My own belief is that tunnels are very emotive places and if one is susceptible to paranormal events a tunnel is just the sort of place for it to happen.

14

THE MYSTERY CHILDREN
AT CHARFIELD

The quiet Gloucestershire village of Charfield was on the main line of the LMS, situated between Gloucester and Bristol. The local station served the surrounding community and carried a fair amount of passenger and freight traffic. The village hit the headlines, however, in a tragic way when an accident and fire happened on 13 October 1928.

The driver of the 10pm LMS passenger and mail train seemingly overran a home signal at danger and plunged into the rear of the 9.15pm Oxley Sidings to Bristol GWR fitted goods before finally colliding with another freight, the 4.45 Westerleigh to Gloucester empties, that was passing on the opposite line.

Interlocking would have prevented the signalman putting the signals for the express at 'CLEAR' yet it is strange that although both footplatemen on the express admitted not having seen the home signal on the approach to Charfield both men were equally emphatic that they had seen the proceeding distant signal and they said it was showing a green light and in the clear position. Immediately following the accident it was discovered that the instrument in Charfield box bore this out and investigation showed that the distant arm was slightly inclined due to debris in the signal wire but not sufficient to show a green light through the spectacle plate.

It is strange therefore that the signal box instruments revealed it as clear, the signal must have been at green, or had a heavy weight been lying across the signal wire? Or again we ask, had the signal been tampered with? The footplatemen had nothing to gain by lying about the position of the distant signal when they admitted not seeing the home signal at all.

The mystery therefore, remains, but it is not the only mystery attached to the Charfield disaster, indeed the one which most concerns us in the context of the strange and uncanny is the riddle of the unclaimed bodies.

Fifteen lives were lost in the accident and the ensuing fire which raged for twelve hours. Two of the dead were children, a girl aged about eight or nine and a boy of about eleven years, they were travelling together, but otherwise unaccompanied. It was alleged that at first the railway company denied that they had been travelling on the train at all, and it was indeed suggested that the two children were chance victims of the holocaust and they happened to be wandering by the railway at the time. However, the evidence of the fireman who was on the footplate of the engine that was hauling the express disproved the allegations of the railway company, for he had seen them together on the train after it had arrived at Birmingham New Street Station around 2.30 when the children had waved at him. He subsequently saw them laughing and talking with the guard before the train left Birmingham and described both youngsters as well dressed; the boy was wearing a school uniform of yellow and brown with cap to match and scarf. Anything else the guard may have remembered is of no value for he was killed in the crash.

In the aftermath of the accident the bodies of the two children were recovered from the wreckage and laid beside the track with the other bodies of the tragedy, but their charred remains were beyond recognition and were never claimed nor was any connection established between them and the other passengers, and in consequence the two children were never identified.

Most of the victims were buried in the village church-yard of St James where the LMS erected a memorial with the names of those laid to rest there. The base of the memorial is inscribed with ten names and the emotive words 'Two Unknown'.

There is even some doubt in some quarters as to whether in fact the unfortunate children were interred at Charfield, for it was said that an Army vehicle was noticed briefly at the scene of the accident, and it has been suggested that some of the remains, possibly those of the children, were removed amid the general confusion.

Someone, somewhere must have been concerned for and worried about these unfortunate children and found their absence odd; surely too, someone must have paid their fare and seen them off on their journey. It is extremely likely, also, that someone was waiting for them at their intended destination.

15

The Mysteries
Of Blea Moor Tunnel

Talk to many a railwayman about the Blea Moor Tunnel and you will find either a spontaneous reaction of a flow of stories or complete and total silence. This bore has a very unpleasant reputation and the local people don't like going near the place at night especially as the rail traffic today has been considerably reduced.

The late Derek Cross had been through the tunnel on the footplate of an A3 Pacific and a Class 40 diesel and on both occasions he had been very pleased to see the other end of the tunnel, such is its evil, brooding, emotive reputation. The construction of the tunnel was very difficult in the Victorian age, men were killed during the excavations, and the depth of 500ft below the surface at one point exposed numerous problems.

Situated below a hill between the valleys of the Ribble and Eden the bore marked the determination of the LMS to refuse to be beaten by obstacles that could be overcome by sheer practical means.

The acrid, choking fumes eventually found their way up through the ventilators on the top of the hill and the height of steam motive power over one hundred trains per day passed through Blea Moor Tunnel. The tremendous build-up of soot on the tunnel roof tended to clog up the apertures of the brick ventilators so a 'blow back' effect was often experienced by footplate crews.

A correspondent, Mr A. W. Kewish of Barrow-in-Furness, Cumbria, tells of his experience in Blea Moor

Tunnel. Mr Kewish wishes to state that neither he nor his wife are psychic.

The Kewishs were on a rail tour over several routes not usually used by passenger trains. The tour was to the Worth Valley, via Blackburn, the Settle and Carlisle, Newcastle and Keighley. What our friends did not realise was that they had to travel through Blea Moor Tunnel. They travelled up the goods line from Blackburn waited for a clear road at Hellifield Junction, got onto the long drag and worked up to the summit. The coaching stock was six or eight a side compartment type with sliding top lights, it was warm in the carriage by the time the tunnel was reached, so a top light was opened. Neither Mr nor Mrs Kewish had any idea what was in Blea Moor Tunnel but they were both very frightened, their one desire was to get off the train as quickly as possible!

They were appalled by the sickly, overpowering, cloying sweet smell that pervaded the carriage, Mr Kewish described it as not dissimilar to incense! Mrs Kewish vowed that she would never, ever travel through Blea Moor Tunnel again. There would appear to be some untold facts about Blea Moor Tunnel as there has been much speculation but very little facts of details. The bore has an evil reputation, whether deserved or not, perhaps because of its lonely location and the emotive nature of a one-and-a-half-mile hole through a hill. Perhaps one day someone in the know will explain in great detail the mysteries of Blea Moor Tunnel.

16

THE BALCOMBE TUNNEL GHOSTS

Train spotting had hardly become an attraction for the boys of the day when the first Easter excursion thundered through Balcombe Tunnel en route to Brighton. It was no ordinary train, but one made up of fifty-seven carriages and hauled by no less than six locomotives that ran the fifty miles from London to the 'Daphne' of the Metropolis, as Brighton has sometimes been called (to quote from *The London Illustrated News* of 7 December 1884); the journey took four and a half hours.

Probably as the snorting monsters emerged from the Black Hole of Balcombe in a cloud of smoke and steam, a merry crowd of villagers who watched from the top of the embankment gave a wary cheer and wondered what the world was coming to! A hundred years on and the scene at Balcombe is much the same; trains faster and far more frequent are still thundering through the tunnel but without the cheering villagers to wave them on their way.

When England was at war and sentries were posted at both ends of the tunnel, one night, early in the war, German planes droned over and dropped bombs along the railway line possibly aiming to destroy the tunnel and so to cut a supply link to the Channel ports and the British armies in France.

Mr E. Myer of Guestling, Sussex, well remembers the night he was on sentry duty from midnight to 2am; several bombs fell close to the tunnel entrance and he decided to take refuge in one of the recesses let into the tunnel walls. After about five minutes he saw a strange sight of

49

what he took to be three men approaching; he challenged them in the usual way and shouted, 'Halt or I fire.' At this the figures became somewhat vague and hazy and then they vanished.

As Mr Myer had been on duty under somewhat arduous conditions for several months he decided that his nerves were playing tricks on him and that he was having hallucinations.

The next day however, on his next tour of duty he met the foreman platelayer when he arrived for work. The latter commented on the air raid and that he never expected to see soldiers guarding the tunnel, especially inside the tunnel for a second time, it having been guarded during World War I. The foreman told him that three soldiers had been killed near the spot that Mr Myer had been in the recess the previous night, they had apparently been run down by a train just inside the tunnel mouth. Today the London to Brighton trains still roar through Balcombe Tunnel, the passengers completely unaware of the tragedy that will haunt the darkened bore for ever.

17

THE STRANGE HAPPENINGS AT INGROW TUNNEL

There are many unexplained events on the Keighley and Worth Valley line that runs from Keighley to Oxenhope five miles further up the branch.

The strange occurrence at Ingrow Tunnel has not been explained by logical reasons and so must be regarded as, maybe, a paranormal phenomenon.

Ingrow Station is at present being rebuilt by the live-ly society that supports the Keighley and Worth Valley Railway Company, as part of a complete refurbishment of the unique branch.

However, the strange events at Ingrow Tunnel take the shape of black smoke billowing out of the tunnel, obviously emanating from a steam locomotive, which is very possible considering the K&WVR has plenty of steam motive power. but on the occasions that we are concerned with none of The Society's locos had been in steam so therefore cannot be blamed for the incident.

Two men, Supervisor D. Narey and his pal Arnold Illingworth, say the smell was remarkably like that of a steam engine. They have investigated the source of the smoke and although they walked the tunnel they have found no explanation except the phenomenon seemed to stop in a recess under the Halifax Road. Another strange point of the mystery is that the two men claimed that the smoke came out of the tunnel mouth towards the station yet a breeze was blowing the other way. Mr Narey ruled out smoke from nearby factories or bonfires in the Wesley Place area. Workers from VOLSEC have spent the last year renovating the Ingrow Station and plan to replace the station buildings next year so I wonder if anything unexplained will be found then?

Railway official Graham Mitchell says the original tunnel builders were plagued with problems including part of the nearby Wesley Chapel sliding away. 'We don't know that anyone was killed or injured near there so there shouldn't be anyone haunting it.'

18

THE GHOST
AT BOX HILL TUNNEL

Box Hill Tunnel is quite a long tunnel, it is in fact one and three quarter miles long, which is a lot of tunnel to maintain for any permanent way gang, whom I don't imagine relish the thought of working in the dark, damp, gloomy bore. It was built by Isambard Kingdom Brunel in 1841 and at the time it was acclaimed as an engineering masterpiece.

To many early rail travellers, however, the gloom of the tunnel was very frightening. They had some very funny ideas about the construction as it was some 300ft below the surface and some of the local people feared the whole land area would collapse. Fears were also expressed by some passengers that the tunnel might collapse while they were travelling through it or that they might suffocate from the lack of air because it was one and three quarter miles long!

However, in the latter days of steam, maintenance workers while near or inside the tunnel were absolutely convinced that they heard the sound of an approaching train. In fact some of them swore that they saw a phantom train roaring into or out of Box Hill Tunnel; of course the sceptics laughed their heads off at such a far-fetched tale but the more psychic were inclined to accept the men's story. Certainly many gangers refused to work in, or near, Box Hill Tunnel, such was the reputation it earned.

Tunnels are so emotive and the mind can conjure up thoughts of terror and the possibility of being run down in a dark tunnel. The mind runs riot at what might happen.

19

FIND THE LADY

Long train journeys are often very boring and tiresome, especially if you are on your own. The monotony is relieved somewhat if you have the opportunity to talk to a fellow traveller who feels the same about long train journeys, then you have something in common besides moaning about the rigours of train travel. Often people who share your compartment wish to relax and do not wish to indulge in polite conversation, they may just want to read a newspaper or magazine so we must respect their wishes.

However, our story concerns a couple, Mr and Mrs Wishart, who in the autumn of 1945 had occasion to visit relatives in Newcastle. The Wisharts, who lived in North London, were not looking forward to the long train journey one little bit; being just after the war, the trains were run down, lacked essential maintenance and didn't keep very good time, so the Wisharts regarded the prospects of the journey with considerable misgivings.

The Wisharts had to catch the 10.30am train from King's Cross and to their amazement they found few people in the usual queue; they had bought newspapers and magazines to read on the journey and when they found an empty compartment they settled down. The windows were fairly clean – well, you could see through them – the layer of dust on the woodwork was thinner than usual and the compartment was reasonably warm.

The train left King's Cross on time and the Wisharts began to read their newspapers, not much conversation took place as they were absorbed with their reading, an occasional smile and a feeling of companionship was enough.

An application of brakes slowed down the clickety-click

of the rail joints. Mr Wishart looked out of the window; they were running through a maze of sidings packed with every kind of rolling stock, the tall chimneys of the brick works dominating the sky line, 'I think this is Peterborough dear,' he remarked. His wife consulted her watch, 'On time too, that is good!' she said. The long train eased into Peterborough Station and the train announcer called 'Peterborough'. A few people were on the platform, the station staff busied themselves with mail bags and other items of luggage and parcels, at last the guard blew his whistle. The Wisharts were about to settle down to their reading when the corridor door slid open and an elderly lady eased her way into the compartment; the newcomer was wearing a striking black silk dress and black hat which were very reminiscent of the Victorian age. The lady was carrying a wicker basket measuring 2ft by 1ft; it was white and to Mrs Wishart it was typical of the lady's attire. The lady smiled and sat down opposite the Wisharts, she carefully placed the wicker basket on the seat next to her, then folded her arms and composed herself in relaxation. The Wisharts resumed their reading, Mrs Wishart kept glancing at the old lady – she couldn't help admiring her dress, it was so Victorian and really out of place in 1945.

The motion of the train, the clickety-click of the rail joints, had a somewhat soporific effect on Mr Wishart and he found himself nodding off. No conversation took place between the three people on the part of the journey between Peterborough and Grantham. Mr Wishart slept and in fact he snored but the old lady was silent, obviously completely composed.

At last the train pulled into Grantham and Mrs Wishart nudged her husband, 'Can you get us a cup of tea, love?' she asked. And in a whisper, 'Perhaps she', looking at the old lady, 'would like one too?' Mr Wishart opened the carriage door and asked a porter how long they had to wait. Had he got time to get a cup of tea? The porter glanced at his watch 'If you hurry sir.' Mr Wishart hurried off to the refreshment room, luckily got served straight away and with difficulty got back to the compartment just as the guard was blowing his whistle; the old lady took one of the paper cups of tea and murmured her thanks.

The Wisharts read the remaining news in their papers and looked out of the window, the old lady was still silent and motionless. The Wisharts kept giving her a look but her eyes were closed and she looked very serene and still.

Eventually Durham was reached and the long train drew into the ancient city. As the brakes came on and the flurry of activity again took in more passengers and luggage the old lady stood up and moved to the door. Mr Wishart stood up and opened it for her, handing her the wicker basket which seemed surprisingly light; the old lady stepped off the train onto a now deserted platform. She turned and said, 'I wish you many happy years'. Then as Mr Wishart was about to say 'Thank you', to his surprise she vanished into thin air. Mr Wishart couldn't believe it. He stepped down onto the platform looking around but there was nowhere she could hide, as if she would! He darted about looking to satisfy his astonishment but the old lady had melted away. The guard blew his whistle, Mr Wishart climbed back into the compartment and sat down. 'Where's she gone, dear?' asked his wife. 'I can't understand it, she just vanished,' he gasped. Then he noticed the third cup with some dregs of tea remaining in it! It hadn't been a dream, or had it?

20

THE REPLAY OF
THE TAY BRIDGE DISASTER

On 28 December 1879 Sir Thomas Bouch's fine example of engineering, the Tay Railway Bridge – over which Queen Victoria had so graciously travelled, pausing on the other side to bestow a knighthood on the brilliant engineer – was overwhelmed by a violent storm, high winds causing the structure to collapse into the foaming river below. Unfortunately, an engine and five coaches were on the bridge at the time and the ninety passengers were drowned.

Local people though, still maintain that every year on the anniversary of the accident, a ghost train crosses the bridge from the Edinburgh side. Its red rear lamp trails into the darkness and finally vanishes . . . just as the Signalman saw the doomed train all those years ago.

The first Tay Bridge showed up the lack of expertise and foresight required for such a structure, no wind tunnels or sophisticated testing were available to the engineers in the late 1870s. Bouch's bridge was made mainly of wrought iron and did not allow for the movement so essential in bridges of that type.

The reappearance of the ill-fated train on the anniversary of the tragedy is not taken lightly by the local inhabitants and there are many people who will vouch for the authenticity of the phenomenon.

21

THE LITTLE OLD GUARD

A strange apparition was witnessed by a lady about two years ago on a section of track between Barking and Upminster in Essex. The lady was travelling on this particular journey which was subject to many delays owing to permanent way maintenance work, and the passengers were heartily fed up with the hassle. Several times they had to step down from the train and walk along the track to the nearest station; on this particular evening the passengers were all wanting to get home and any delay was not welcome.

Our lady who kindly offered me her account of the happenings was returning home from a hospital visit. It was around 6pm, very dark; suddenly the train began to slow down to a crawl, 'what now?' thought the passengers. Then to everyone's surprise they saw on the side of the track a little old man perhaps in his seventies, wearing an old-fashioned waistcoat and jacket, standing in a brick arch-shaped embrasure looking anxiously at the train. As we drew near he took a step forward shining his lantern with its green light above his head as if to give the driver the 'All Clear'. Our correspondent smiled to herself, no doubt thinking that the railway company must be short of staff if they had to bring such an old man out of his back garden to work the system.

Since that occasion my correspondent has tried to find the embrasure or refuge that the old man was standing in, without success. It simply isn't there, even the wall doesn't exist. The whole scene to my informant was as clear as a bell, but on reflection it would seem as if it was part of an earlier railway system. She is absolutely confident that she was privileged to witness a scene from the past in startling clarity that would continue to baffle her for ever.

22

TULSE HILL STATION

Mr Jack Hallam's excellent book *Ghosts of London* tells of the unexplained sounds of heavy footsteps heard by staff at night at Tulse Hill Station. Footsteps are heard ascending the stairs to platform 1 passing clean through the locked barrier gates and proceeding along the platform.

The footsteps are said to be those of an unfortunate platelayer who was killed shortly after the introduction of the electric trains. On the fateful night he ascended the stairs, passed through the barrier and greeted the porter on duty and then he walked down onto the track. It was a blustery, windy, cold night and knowing that a down steam-hauled train was due, he stepped onto the up line instead of the safety of the trackside cess. It is thought that the sound of the approaching steam train and the prevailing gale prevented him from being aware of the electric train's presence.

He was run down and killed, but he was so attached to his job that he still wants to keep his eye on his old work place. Today certain people will not go on the station after dark, so the past tragedy lingers on over an entire railway complex.

23

CUBBAGE FROM THE PLAIN

This is a story of a misunderstanding that reduced a man to suicide, also the love affair that fell foul of the postal system and tragic circumstances, the combined forces of fate culminating in the tragedy. The lady concerned is left completely distraught, and a restless, searching ghost that never finds peace and affection.

Mr Cubbage was an Indian, dark, and very handsome. He had settled in Ireland many years ago and through his shrewd business ability and financial acumen he had become very wealthy.

Just after World War II he bought a large mansion 'on the Plain' and restored it to its prior magnificent glory and settled down to enjoy his wealth. There was only one thing he lacked and that was a wife. Mr Cubbage must have seemed a good catch with his fine house, handsome looks and with his obvious wealth. Could any girl resist these assets?

Mr Cubbage, however, was very circumspect in his choice of lady friends and he realised that he could be the target for any gold-digging female. He looked around very carefully and finally met a young lady with whom he fell head-long in love. Their mutual affection was genuine and Mr Cubbage was overjoyed at his good fortune; he entertained his young lady, who we will call Coleen, to the best things in life. He heaped presents of jewellery, furs, motor cars, travel, expensive restaurants, days out hunting, on her; in other words Mr Cubbage was trying to sweep the young lady clean off her pretty feet.

Mr Cubbage wanted to get married without further delay. Coleen, however, although she loved Mr Cubbage, wanted time to think things over and would gently scold him for his haste. Coleen listened to his amorous overtures of love never doubting his sincerity, but she still wanted to be sure and she tried to gently tell him so; she had to be sure before she said 'yes'.

Her lover, however, was not to be put off. He wanted an answer quickly, he wasn't used to delay of any kind and kept up the pressure, 'Please give me your answer,' he implored. And he pressed his suit so forcibly yet kindly. He loved Coleen with all the breath in his body, he would do anything to please her to be his wife. Coleen was not going to be rushed and after a lot of thought she decided to go to stay with friends in England to think things over.

Mr Cubbage was like a cat on hot bricks, he was most distraught at Coleen's decision to go to England, and he bombarded her with letters and flowers; he could not wait for her return and for her to say the one word that would make her his wife.

Coleen however, was enjoying herself in England, she thought of Mr Cubbage a lot but thought she wouldn't commit herself just yet. Mr Cubbage was by this time almost demented, he had to know Coleen's decision, so he wrote an impassioned letter begging her to accept his proposal of marriage. Furthermore, he added what would be construed as an ultimatum but couched in the nicest possible terms. He wrote his plea as follows: if he hadn't had a reply from her before noon on the last day of the week (which meant return post) he would trouble her no more.

The first delivery of post came and went on that fateful day, no letter. Mr Cubbage, his heart heavy with disappointment and sadness, left his mansion and walked the short distance to the main Portadown to Lurgan railway line and awaited the passing of the next train. He walked up and down the track, waiting impatiently; he had made his mind up, he was going to lie down in front of the train. His life was meaningless without Coleen, she had not replied to his entreaties so he would end it all.

He heard the train whistle, the engine was slowing for a signal then he heard it pick up speed again. Mr Cubbage, now a broken, weeping figure lay down on the rail and waited for the train to end his life and his earthly troubles. The driver of the train didn't see him until it was too late, the engine literally cut him in half, he must have died instantly.

The next part of the story is pure circumstance but the effect might have saved poor Mr Cubbage's life.

That particular day's sailings between England and Ireland were delayed owing to bad weather so the mail was accountably held up and delays caused. It so happened that the very train that ended Mr Cubbage's life was carrying the delayed mail and in one of the mail bags was a letter from Coleen agreeing to Mr Cubbage's proposal of marriage and saying that she was coming home to her lover.

The ghost of Mr Cubbage walks the coaches of many trains searching for his beloved Coleen; he has been seen often by many people in the district, he also walks the railway tracks near the spot on which he was killed, a sobbing, totally heart-broken figure. He is said to sink onto his knee on the track and wait for the train to end his life; the train crews used to look out for the shadowy figure and shudder.

The tragedy of the whole affair becomes so pathetic as we realise that Coleen does love him and only a delay of post cost him his life.

24

THE SUICIDAL STUDENT & CO

About the turn of the century, a young medical student, who was studying at Aberdeen University, ran into financial difficulties. His father, a well-to-do fish merchant in Fraserburgh, had no idea of a student's expenses at a university like Aberdeen. Ian Watson, the student in question was a clever young man who had worked very hard to achieve his place at the higher seat of learning; he found it very difficult to manage on the pittance that his father allowed him. His father's idea of universities was narrow in the extreme and possibly based on his own education which had been one of strict discipline and the basic three Rs; he had left school at thirteen and had to work hard for very little reward. Give him credit though, he had fought his way to the top and had made good.

Ian Watson was a dedicated, somewhat highly strung young man whose intelligence would have enabled him to have passed his final exams had his father realised that a reasonable allowance was so necessary. His father obviously didn't appreciate his son's undoubted abilities. His son's request for more money met with scorn 'Come home and work with me, lad, don't mess about with them books, I need you here,' his father said.

Ian was very upset by his father's intransigent attitude but he knew what he wanted to do and that was to pursue his studies by every means possible, although by now doubts were beginning to cloud his mind.

Inevitably a feeling of despair enveloped him and he began to feel quite helpless; his heart was in his studies and he knew that if he could manage financially he could achieve his academic rewards, but the insufficient amounts of money his father allowed him didn't permit any freedom to relax after his studies had ended. He could see no way out and in his anguish he began to think of doing himself in; the method he would use would have to be quick and simple. After some consideration he decided that he would lie on the railway line and let a train end his life; he remembered a high bridge over the railway at Kirkston of Philorth, that would do.

He decided to throw himself off the parapet of the bridge instead of lying down on the track. He would time it just right and throw himself in front of the branch line train, he knew the train didn't go very fast but it would do . . .

In the early evening of the next day he dressed himself in his best suit and wore a clean shirt and a razor tight collar; he looked at himself in the mirror, yes, he looked good, almost handsome, one must die with dignity.

He had quite a long way to walk to the bridge, but there was plenty of time; he had taken the trouble to find out the train times and he had worked out at what time the train would arrive at the bridge – about 9pm – so he enjoyed his walk. He arrived at the bridge, walked over it then back again, he looked over the parapet at the shining metals, the line curved away round a curve; he looked around, everything was quiet, the moon had come out and there was just a touch of frost in the air. Ian climbed up onto the parapet and sat swinging his legs humming a tune; he felt quite happy now, almost cheerful, thoughts came to him, why was he thinking of suicide? He had everything to live for really, he would manage on the money his mean father allowed him. He began to sing softly, should he go through with his intention to end his life? 'That's what I'm here for,' an inner voice shouted. 'Don't be silly, why do something stupid like hurling yourself in front of a train,' the thoughts crowded his mind. He looked at his pocket watch, it showed 8.55pm, not long to go now; he was in a turmoil of doubt, what should he do? He found a cigarette, lit it and watched the smoke wreathe into the night air; he enjoyed his smoke, then climbed onto the parapet and started to walk along its broad surface. He would walk over and back then go home, life was still sweet in spite of father's mean ways. He could hear the muffled sound of the train as it plodded round the curves. Ian, happier now, ran and danced on the parapet, 'Come on train, I'm not afraid of you.' The train rumbled nearer, Ian was still jigging about on the parapet, he could see the smoke box lamp flickering, then as the train was almost on the bridge the smoke enveloped the structure as Ian was doing his Highland jig; he suddenly lost his balance and fell down onto the smoke box frame, the force of the fall did its lethal work and killed Ian Watson.

The train braked hard at the fireman's shout, 'There's a man on the line.' The few passengers on the train were thrown from their seats as Walt the driver braked hard. The driver and fireman ran up to the inert body; too late, the man was dead. His head was at a strange angle. They carried the body to the brake compartment and carried on their journey; others had jumped from that bridge and there would be more.

The unfortunate tragedy was a talking point in the district for several weeks but then slowly receded into the aeons of time. Then a reminder of the tragedy came during World War I when a Polish soldier was walking over the bridge one starlit night when he saw the wraith of a man dancing on the parapet. Then smoke obscured the bridge and a sound of escaping steam and a cry took the man out of the observer's sight. The soldier looked over the parapet and saw to his horror the vague heap of a body; he scrambled down the bank but as he approached, the vision slowly faded, there was no one there. This experience had such a dramatic effect on the Pole that he hanged himself some days later.

No further reports have been documented, but possibly people who have seen a replay of the awful scene wish to remain silent not wishing to discuss the macabre subject. In the 1920s a local man was in a terrible state of nerves and he too visited the bridge with the one thought in his mind. Yes, he did commit suicide on that bridge but he drank from a bottle of lysol which would mean a swift but painful end. I wonder if he is seen too?

25

THE HIGH WYCOMBE FOOTSTEPS

A recent story, quite unexplained, was related to me by Mr G. Leslie who is employed by British Rail in the London area.

This story concerns the sounds of footsteps walking in the ballast; no one was seen but the sounds were very convincing and one respects the account of this mystery from Mr Leslie, who certainly didn't believe in the supernatural, preferring to find a logical explanation of this sort of thing.

However, when telling his experience to a member of the High Wycombe Station staff he found that his experience was certainly not unprecedented.

Mr Leslie had been to a railway staff party in a pub called the Flint, which is situated across the road from High Wycombe Station. Mr Leslie admits to having had a drink but he says he was by no means 'under the influence'. At about 11.20pm he left the party to catch his train back to his home at Beaconsfield.

As a northbound train had just left, the station was deserted. Mr Leslie's train was to leave platform 3 on the far left-hand side of the station which is linked by a long subway. On arriving on platform 3 somewhat early for his train, he found himself completely alone; this did not disturb him.

The night was still but a mist was descending slowly; he stood looking towards platforms 2 and 1 when he suddenly heard footsteps on the ballast approaching him. As Mr Leslie had explained earlier he was completely sober and was not given to imagination, he screwed his eyes up looking for the reason for the footsteps; he couldn't see the feet but heard them quite distinctly passing him in the ballast below. At this point some other people arrived to catch the train and his attention turned to them for a split second and within that time the sound of the scrunching footsteps disappeared into the night.

Sometime later, after Christmas, Mr Leslie was on High Wycombe Station again and was talking to one of the station staff. He told him of his experience and was interested to know that the phenomenon is by no means unknown and the other went on to relate another incident involving footsteps that he heard outside the office, but when he opened the door to investigate no one was there.

On another occasion he gave chase to someone running down the platform but when he reached the platform end whoever it was or wasn't had vanished. He was certain that he was dealing with a facet of the supernatural now!

26

THE MYSTERY LIGHTS

Paranormal experiences never happen to some people. That is why they can't understand other people who are able to experience supernatural events. Research has only scratched the surface of the paranormal and supernatural phenomena, so we are left with odd cases of happenings that just materialise when least expected.

Such an occurrence happened to Mr R. J. Woodward of Ninckley and his wife and daughter when travelling home around midnight along the Watling Street (A5). They had been visiting friends, they had enjoyed their evening and the time had gone quickly so it was rather late when they set off for home.

They had negotiated the roundabout for Lutterworth and the A427 to Coventry and were proceeding north on the A5 when Mr Woodward's attention was suddenly drawn to what he first thought were three buses stood nose to tail. Before he could say anything Mrs Woodward exclaimed 'Isn't it strange to see a train at this time of night?' Mr Woodward knew the area well and there were no railways here at all; there used to be many years ago and there are still signs of the old trackbed to be seen.

Mr Woodward, being something of a railway buff, couldn't help thinking that the lights were spread out as in the old non-corridor stock, three windows to each compartment, but there was no vague outline of a loco-motive, just the lights, no shape of the carriages.

The low line was closed about thirty years ago but there was never a track just where the lights were positioned; distance is deceptive especially at night, there might have been a branch line, but maybe not?

The phenomenon lasted perhaps thirty to forty-five seconds, long enough for a lasting impression to be gained but the phenomenon was very clear and distinct leaving the Woodwards very puzzled by the unexpected sight.

Mr Woodward's map of the position helps to illustrate the location of the event.

27

GHOSTS
IN A RECORDING STUDIO

The Horizon Recording Studio is housed in an old Victorian railway building in Warwick Road, Coventry.

A series of strange events have happened in the building which can be traced to the ghost of an old railwayman, and more recently the spirit of an art student who unfortunately got hooked on hard drugs, which combined with drink killed him after he had attended the celebration party to launch the Horizon Recording Studio. This young man died about ten years ago and the railwayman maybe thirty years before.

Mr Paul Craddock who is a director of Horizon has kindly sent me some details of the paranormal events that have earned the studio a certain reputation for experiences of the, shall we say, 'unexpected'. Certainly some famous recording artists have had some frightening moments when they have been nudged and brushed past by these two ghosts.

The young art student was about nineteen when he died; he had worked hard on the dramatic murals in the studio and then he tried mixing drugs with drink and that was fatal. The studio was once part of a railway company property and that is where the old railwayman comes in. He probably worked here and certainly his presence is very evident. The strong feeling of a presence is felt, lights go on and off, doors open and shut on their own, the shadow of a man's head is sometimes seen; but on recording sessions, many unnerving things can happen, heavy breathing down the musicians' necks, brushing past people. Footsteps are

heard all over the building causing surprise and appre-
hension and expectancy in those visitors who have heard
about the phenomena but haven't experienced it.

Strange sounds are heard live over the loud speaker
monitors, some times spoiling the recordings. A famous
recording artist with the group Fleetwood Mac was really
frightened by one of the duo and he swears that he will
never come into the building again such was his experience.

As with most supernatural occurrences one never
knows just when something is going to happen and this is
the case in the studio. A recording session can be spoilt
completely by these two ghosts. Mr Craddock thinks
that the older man is dominating the art student. The
directors are probably used to the supernatural events
that happen from time to time; the very fact that the
building has connections with the railways has possibly
something to do with the old railwayman but in what
context I do not know.

28

THE NEWTY POND MOTORBIKE

This story concerns two young boys who came across the reoccurrence of a terrible death involving a young irresponsible lad who used to play 'chicken' with a motor-cycle on an ungated railway crossing. This lethal game is often called 'last across', the idea being to see how close you can be to a train before it hits you or you can get out of the way.

Of course, at last a train got him and killed him in a horrible way. On one very hot night in June 1982 Dave and Tony went fishing in a rather remote area of wasteland that bordered a disused railway line. A large pond was the boys' delight and they would travel the considerable distance to the 'newty' pond, as it was nicknamed, to sit in expection for the fish to bite. The pond was situated in an area that necessitated walking though two dark, gloomy plantations that after dark were very spooky and the boys were always pleased to get through them.

However, boys will be boys and they enjoyed the fresh air and the sport of fishing, in fact the boys had been known to fish after dark at the newty pond which was very illegal! But the fishing trip that hot night was something different and it was to frighten and distress the boys.

They found their usual post at the pond and set up their gear; it was hot and very humid, they were near the gated level crossing on the old trackbed. Nothing much doing at the pond, they had set the rods up and were wandering around, looking for frogs and newts, then they returned to their rods; nothing stirred, so around 10pm they decided to call it a day. They got their rods and landing nets together and set off for home. All of a sudden they heard the hum of a motorcycle coming towards them and they both saw a motorcycle being ridden towards the level crossing. It was travelling at high speed and the boys thought it was going to hit them, the rider was crouched over the bars obviously unaware of the boys. They threw down their fishing gear and ran as the motorcycle leapt over the embankment and crashed into the deep ditch some 15ft below. The boys heard the crash and they ran as fast as they could to get help from the police and ambulance, but when the police and ambulance got there they only found the boys' fishing tackle where they had dumped it in such haste.

The boys never went to the pond again but did hear reports from other anglers that screams and shouts came from the ditch the other side of the old trackbed, also the eerie, noisy sound of a motorcycle being ridden flat out towards the railway line.

About a year later one of the boys met an old lady who lived not far from the pond and they were discussing the strange happenings when the lady said, 'I can tell you a bit about it,' and she then proceeded to tell them about the crazy motorcyclist. 'He was mad on motorbikes and he would tear around on that wasteland near the railway, bent on killing himself, I'd say. He'd play last across with the trains, no wonder he was killed by a train, he had many near misses, he always appears on the anniversary of his death and you would see the whole incident in startling detail.'

I understand that the deep ditch that the boy and motorcycle crashed into on that fateful night is referred to as 'deadman's ditch', a horrific reminder of a foolhardy game that cost a young man his life. One of the boys, now adult, tells me that even today he shivers at the thought that is etched on his brain of being chased by a ghost on a motorcycle . . .

29
DICKY O' TUNSTEAD

The legend relating to Dicky o'Tunstead caused the London North Western Railway Company many problems and succeeded in forcing this railway company to reconsider their plans for their new line between Chapel-en-le-Frith and Buxton.

Dicky o' Tunstead is a celebrated skull who lived at Tunstead Farm in Derbyshire for some three and a half centuries. He found fame in poetry and prose, he also has the reputation of being a supernatural Robin Hood and documentary evidence of his exploits attributed to him are legion.

Suffice it to say that all attempts to evict Dicky from his rightful home have met with considerable misfortune, and disturbance of such a nature that he has quickly been restored to his home.

Tunstead Farm overlooks Coomb Reservoir between Chapel-en-le-Frith and Whaley Bridge. The LNWR's engineers had planned to take their new line across land belonging to the farm, despite objections from the owners, and this is where Dicky became involved.

It was originally intended to make an embankment across the Coomb Valley which was to be pierced by a bridge to accommodate a roadway. Soon after work began however, it was found that there were serious problems in making a secure, stable base for the embankment and thus progress was brought to a halt.

Eventually, however, the navvies and engineers overcame the difficulties and the bridge was erected over the road and the foundations of the embankment were laid. Then before work was finally complete the arch of the bridge collapsed and the embankment at either side of the bridge was thrown up thus wrecking the whole project. A lot of time and money had been spent rebuilding the works necessary to complete the job but such were the difficulties experienced that the whole project became completely impracticable and the LNWR conceded defeat and altered the route of the line to exclude the land at Tunstead Farm.

The new work also involved the construction of a road over a quarter of a mile long but no unexpected difficulties were experienced, either with this or the re-aligned route of the railway.

Of course the sceptics and the doubters will sneer at the influence on the affair exercised by Dicky saying that the former route was unsuitable and geographically unstable, and they will point out that such conditions have been overcome in other parts, for example, the West Highland, the Liverpool and Manchester and the Settle and Carlisle, but then those conversant with Dicky o' Tunstead will continue to believe that it is his malign influence which kept the rails away from Tunstead Farm.

30

THE 'LUCK' OF EDENHALL

A legend concerning the London North Western Railway Company 'Whitworth' class locomotive named *The Luck of Edenhall* No 90 – what an unusual name – but then the story of how it came by the name is unusual too.

The name is derived from Eden Hall, a mansion which stands near Penrith and curiously enough within sight of the Settle and Carlisle line of the Midland Railway. Eden Hall was the family seat of the Cumbrian family of Musgrave since the days of King Henry VI; the 'Luck' is an heirloom, a beautifully enamelled and engraved glass goblet with Moorish-style decorative work on its surfaces.

How it came into the Musgrave family is as follows.

The family butler went to draw water from St Cuthbert's well in the grounds of Eden Hall one day when he came across a company of fairies dancing, and in their midst was a cup of painted glass.

The butler seized the glass where upon the fairies tried to regain the cup but realising that they were no match for this mortal they finally abandoned the struggle and vanished, leaving the butler with the glass cup and according to a ballad by the German poet Uhland with this warning.

If that glass either break or fall
Farewell to the Luck of Eden Hall

Ever since that time, the fate of the Musgrave family and the strangely beautiful glass goblet have been regarded as inextricably entwined. The vessel is described as being about six inches tall and it has been suggested that it may have been used as a chalice, and it might have originated in Spain or Syria and been brought home to England from one of the Crusades. But whatever the origins the fairy folk warning has never been left to chance and the 'Luck' still exists; it is either locked away in a strong room on the premises or according to some accounts stored safely in the custody of the Bank of England. Eden Hall was extensively rebuilt in 1935 or thereabouts, and much of the original fabric removed at that time, today it is a girls' school.

The poet Longfellow's version of the Uhland ballad runs thus,

This Glass of Flashing Crystal Tall
Gave to my Sires, The Fountain Sprite
She wrote in it, 'If this Glass Doth Fall
Farewell Then Luck of Eden Hall'

It is from the last line of this work that the LNWR coined the name for their locomotive.

31

THE SPECTRAL TRAIN
OF KYLE!

Some supernatural manifestations are regarded as portents of good or evil; one such occurrence was the Spectral Train of Kyle. In the seventeenth century a famous visionary and seer, locally know as the Brahan Seer, predicted 'That the day will come when every stream will have its bridge, balls of fire will pass rapidly up and down the Strath of Peffery, carriages without horses will cross the country from sea to sea.' This prophecy came true when in 1870 the Dingwall & Skye Railway opened its line from Dingwall on the eastern seaboard to Strome Ferry on the west on the shores of the waters of Loch Carron.

A further twenty-seven years were to elapse before the railway reached its ultimate terminus at the Kyle of Lochalsh. However, the imminent arrival of the railway was foreshadowed by an appearance of a spectral train whose large black locomotive was seen rushing along the lonely Highland road with headlights blazing before suddenly veering off into the hills. It would seem that this apparition became a regular occurrence to such an extent that the coachman who operated a public conveyance until the opening of the railway to Kyle of Lochalsh would only run in daylight.

32

FRENCH DROVE AND GEDNEY HILL

This station was opened by the GNR on 2 September 1867 and in 1882 the operating company became part of the GN&GE Joint Railway Company. Situated south of Postland (Crowland) on the Spalding to March line near the point where the GN line crossed the M&GN joint line at Murrow, refuge sidings were a facility at this station, to handle a considerable volume of freight traffic, mainly generated by local farmers with their produce. Passenger traffic was profitable until BR decided that this facility should be withdrawn on 11 September 1961, but the goods traffic continued until the ultimate closure of the station on 5 October 1964.

This quaintly named station was a victim of the Beeching Axe, and after closure of the station is was offered for sale as a dwelling house. The line was still open but run down and neglected, with fewer and fewer trains travelling over the weed-covered rusting tracks. After a while, general deterioration having started, a buyer was found. Mr Harold Caunt and his son moved in to restore the structure and make it into a home.

The Caunts, however, were to experience several unwanted and totally unexpected events which were to bewilder and baffle them, but let Mr Caunt explain the strange events.

'One fine day, being in need of provisions, my eldest son Terry and I cycled to the village shop in Gedney Hill. While being served by the young lady behind the counter, who had noticed that we were strangers, we were asked from whence we came. 'French Drove station,' we replied. On hearing our reply she went deathly white. 'Oh dear,' she said eventually, 'you don't want to live there, the place is haunted.'

'Now being of a practical disposition and having lived in many strange places I wasn't going to be put off by local village rumours about ghosts. We carried on the restoration work at the station; there was much to do and we were kept very busy and involved with our work.

'Subsequent events, however, were to remind us of the shop girl's warning. The mail in those days was delivered by a post lady on a bike and was usually delivered at around 8.30am. One day we were having breakfast when we heard a woman's voice from near the foot of the stairs in the hall. Expecting to find the post lady at the door Terry went to collect the mail only to find no one in view. He looked around but there was no sign of anyone. Puzzling, he returned to report, 'No one there'.

'It so happened that the post was late that day. We considered the events carefully, as we certainly did not consider ourselves as fools nor did we imagine things of this nature. We had definitely heard a woman's voice, that was certain, so we had to accept the fact that something funny was going on and we would have to see what happened in the future.

'Some time later we had a visit from a young man who worked for BR and was on holiday revisiting some of the stations that he had worked at in the past. During a conversation in which I mentioned the mystery of the woman's voice, he explained that many years ago a stationmaster at French Drove committed suicide by hanging himself from a hook in the ceiling of the room above the ticket office. His poor, distressd wife died shortly afterwards and it transpired that she used to help her husband in his duties. It became her job to close the station at night, and in the dark winter nights she used to carry a stable lantern to enable her to find her way around the dark corners of the station. Our visitor told us that her ghost had been seen by several local people at certain times of the year. So, when a lighted lamp wobbled along the track one dark, winter's night, we really cringed in terror. Luckily there was an explanation for this occurrence. We found that the husband of the crossing keeper further up the line – who worked at Perkin's engines – would ride his bike along the track when on his night shift, up on to the platform and leave it under the signal box to await his transport to work; hence the wobbly light.

'However, the mystery of the woman's voice remained a worrying event that often caused a shiver to run down our spines. Also, the stories of the sighting of the ghost of the stationmaster's wife were confirmed by the local residents, many of whom wouldn't come near the station after dark. So what now? Let us hope that the restless ghost of a distraught wife has found peace at last, certainly no logical reason has been offered to explain the strange events at French Drove and Gedney Hill station and it will continue to baffle and tantalise our enquiring minds for some time to come.'

33

THE 'UNSEEN' TRAIN
AT REDDITCH

To refer to the unmistakable sound of a train 'working hard against the grade', ethereal or paranormal, is open to debate but that is what my correspondent Mr Bernard Essex heard one early morning. As Mr Essex observes, to make up a convincing faked ghost story is difficult but to tell the incredible truth is easy because this incredible experience Mr Essex tells me is absolutely true.

Mr Essex lives in the Warwickshire village of Studley and about one mile east of the former trackbed of the railway that ran from Redditch in a generally southerly direction towards Alcester, Evesham and Ashchurch. Now all rail services south of Redditch were terminated in June 1964 and until that time Mr Essex could hear quite clearly the sound of trains from his house, most of them were steam hauled when the services ceased in June 1964. Naturally when the services ended the familiar sounds were no more, just a memory. But were they? About three months after the final operation, at about 6am one morning, Mr Essex was getting up, he was wide awake and dressing. All was still and quiet, when suddenly on the early morning breeze came the faint sound of a steam locomotive on the now closed railway line, working hard with a sharp cut off as it fought the familiar gradient. Mr Essex was utterly amazed and quickly opened the window to investigate.

The sound came louder to a final familiar crescendo then it died away gradually to a faint whisper, then it had gone as if it had been proceeding normally on its journey.

Mr Essex assures me that the exhaust beats were clearly audible, the sounds of steam issuing from the cylinder drain cocks and the clank in the valve gear were clearly heard. the experience lasted for about three minutes.

Later that day, Mr Essex phoned Redditch Station to ask the staff about the possibility of trains running on the aforementioned line northward to Birmingham and Mr Essex told them what he had heard. Eventually he spoke to the station master who was very interested yet amused by the story. The station master explained that although the track south of Redditch was still in situ, all the points and control to single-line working and exit at the south end had been taken out and it would have been impossible for a train to leave or enter Redditch at that end.

Mr Essex of course searched for a logical explanation of this mystery; the only other operating part of British Railways in the area was and still is the Great Western line at Henley-in-Arden. This line runs about eight miles to the east of Mr Essex's home and Mr Essex assures me that it is completely inaudible, so we can discard that theory.

Even a practical joker playing back a recording of a steam train operating over that line would have to be very clever to produce a conclusive effect especially from a static position.

Mr Essex was, he believes, the only person who heard the unexplained sounds and he says although his experience cannot be corroborated he believes that there would be no point in making up such a story.

So we are left with the mysterious sounds that would seem to provide no rational explanation.

34

THE STRATEGIC RESERVE, FACT OR FICTION?

Where did all the steam locomotives go? As the sixties drew to a close the remaining workhorses of British Railways became increasingly grimy, run down and leaked steam from every joint. The majority went to scrapyards but the lucky few were rescued by the preservation movement and although in serious states of dilapidation were restored in many cases, and now earn their keep on the increasing number of preserved lines.

However, rumours persist these days that a certain number of steam locomotives had been extensively over-hauled at BR's works and stored away in remote parts of the British Isles to provide motive power in the case of an emergency. If we remember the long shed at Hartlepool's motive power depot with its two round houses where the once large fleet of engines were coaled, watered, and serviced between duties; one day they were there, next day they were gone, stored to await their fate.

In those days steam depots were depressing places and locomotives were seen in forlorn convoys being hauled away to the scrapyards. Albert Draper's yard was full of these sad, forgotten, rusting steel hulks as they waited to be broken up by the cutter's torch to be eventually recycled into razor blades or motor cars. Yet there are tales and theories to support the notion that not all the discarded steamers met such an ignoble fate. The sudden cut back in oil to British Railways and other users in 1979, which was about ten per cent, and of brief duration, fed the fabled strategic reserve rumour, especially as now the world is awash with oil!

The idea of a huge store of locomotives in a camouflaged shed or a tunnel complex beneath a mountain awaiting the call to come to Britain's rescue in a time of national crisis has all the hallmarks of King Arthur and his knights of the round table slumbering until danger threatens their kingdom. For the chivalrous sleeping heroes to be wakened by the call of a horn, imagine instead the familiar chime whistle of an A4 surging along and the emotive effect engendered in that simple act.

We will therefore look at the arguments one by one and assess their merits and real possibilities and seek the tell-tale signs that suggest contrary beliefs.

Where did all the locomotives go?

The answer to this in the majority of cases must be the scrapyards, apart from those bought for private preservation and now operating privately. Rhyd-y-mynm near Mold in North Wales is thought to be a location for a number of the strategic reserve. It is believed to be a complex of small buildings surrounded by a perimeter fence with security guards and has been noted by certain eagle-eyed people. There were ventilator shafts in the mountain to suggest underground chambers, rail connected to British Railways. Until the early seventies the track has been partially lifted but there remains a section continuing from Mold almost to its doorstep without apparent reason.

Another choice is Hessay near York, the home of the 322 Engineers Park Royal Engineers. Here tracks ran between prefabricated buildings with a link to British Railways' York and Harrogate line; army depots at Bicester, Oxon and Marchwood, Hampshire are other choices. The War Department has revealed that at each depot there are locomotives . . . but they are all diesels employed for the movement of stores. Marchwood speculation was boosted when it was revealed that David Shepherd's 9F *Black Prince* was overhauled in this depot albeit a high security heavily guarded complex. A comment from a letter written to the magazine *Steam Railway* was as such: 'It would be interesting to guess what equipment exists at Marchwood that could retube a 9F in 1979.' Maybe closed guarded doors, barbed wire and a lot of emotive ideas created the sort of situation of James Bond fantasies!

Which locomotives may have been retained?

The obvious choice would be those of the BR standard classes constructed under the modernisation plan, with the various types including the maximum amount of interchangeable fittings to provide maintenance economies. Built between 1951 and 1960 many 9Fs had had only nine years' service before withdrawal. Records have been kept by individuals and the RCTS through its magazine *Railway Observer* of withdrawals and dispersal points; only a handful of standards are not accounted for. There are of course a large number of locomotives of all sizes active in private hands; are these the ones that would be commandeered in the case of emergency?

Could a steam reserve still function?

The answer is certainly yes. The current number of steam excursions running on BR suggests so, removal of water troughs and columns, coaling towers and the other hardware have been successfully bypassed. Steam crews are still available, in fact BR have been training drivers and firemen to cope with the excellent business that has been generated by steam specials, coupled with the fact that BR have been busy 'thinning out' the mainline diesel classes in recent years and are always grumbling about 'lack of motive power'.

I have heard of many reports of where redundant steam locomotives may be stored. Some of the reports are highly credible, some are pure fantasy. It is not impossible for the strategic reserve to exist, remember the emotive report in the magazine *Steam Railway* – one old driver recalls an unusual tale. One Sunday, he had just come off the shed with a train of 'old scrappers' when he was stopped at a signal box. The signalman explained that he had received 'fresh instructions', the driver and fireman were to be relieved and another crew took over. The could still expect full pay, they never saw the train or whoever took it over. Here we see the mysterious interruption of journey, full pay, unexpected time off and a strange disappearance.

However, regarding the strategic reserve, there are no supporting documents, no unimpeachable testimonies, and no photographs to give the rumour credibility. Government sources have of course never divulged the location of certain important emergency measures and in the case of the hidden store of steam locomotives this blanket of security is essential. The railway enthusiast will search and try to find out whether the rumour is fact or fiction. But I hope that the mystery will be discussed at all levels, but only as a talking point, so we can only wonder and imagine a line of standard class locomotives in first class condition waiting for the chance to show the modern motive power a thing or two!

35

SECOND SIGHT?

I am indebted to Mr M. Houghton of Bolton for a very strange mystery that he was to experience during his boyhood but to this day there would appear to be no explanation. One can only think that he somehow became involved in a kind of time warp that was to bewilder him some thirty years later.

It happened when he was thirteen, and very keen on train spotting; he would, like most boys of his age, go anywhere to get engine numbers. He was an expert on the different types of engines, where they came from, where they were going to and in fact anything to do with trains the lad knew all about it. This incident took place in 1950, it was a Sunday evening in August and the location was Northenden Junction on the Cheshire lines where the main line into Stockport (Tiviot Dale) and the branch into Stockport (Edgely) diverged.

'On this particular Sunday, as on most Sundays, the signal box at Northenden Junction was switched out and the signals left clear for the main line to and from Tiviot Dale. The next box to the west (Baguley) was apparently switched out – it invariably was on a Sunday – and the distant signal was showing clear for the whole of the time that I was at the location. This left a very long section of line between Skelton Junction to the west, which in my recollection was always open and I think Heaton Mersey to the east (towards Stockport Tiviot Dale). As I was aware that excursions to and from the Lancashire coast very often passed through Northenden on a Sunday, I cycled along there to see whether there would be any action, I positioned myself on a road bridge adjacent to Northenden Junction Signal Box. It was a very clear summer evening, visibility was excellent and there was full light. I waited on the bridge for about an hour, I was very patient but now began to fidget. I wanted to see some action, besides I had to be home soon as I had a paper round to do early the following morning. No one was about, I looked up and down the line, nothing in sight. I was just about to pack up and go home when I suddenly saw the smoke of a train approaching from the direction of Skelton Junction. I positioned myself on the bridge parapet, safely of course, to get a good look at the engine and the length of the train.

'When it came into view, the engine was a Stanier Class 5, or Black Five as the train spotters called them. It was hauling a train of five coaches and when it reached my position I noted the engine's number on the smoke box door as 44813. It was travelling at a leisurely pace, probably between 40 and 45 mph. I paid no more attention to it as it passed under the bridge but recorded the number in my pocket book that I always carried with me on these trips.

'I then looked up and down the line to see if anything else was in sight and noticed to my surprise another plume of smoke coming from the same direction as the other train. I quickly looked to see if I could see the last train but of course it had disappeared. I couldn't believe that two trains should follow each other so close, but it was another train all right and I was interested to see if it was another passenger working.

'Although at my tender age I did not understand the complexities of signalling something told me that all was not as it should be but by now the train was getting nearer and I was bent on taking the number of the loco.

'I remained in my position on the bridge and as the train approached I saw that it was again a Stanier Black Five hauling five carriages, same as the last one. Now for the number; again I peered at the smoke box number plate, to my surprise it read 44813. I was puzzled, the train was running again leisurely at between 40 and 45mph, same as the last one, I thought, very strange! I opened my pocket book, there on the page was the number of the previous train, 44813, I couldn't believe it. It would appear that I had been caught up in something queer at that time, the thought of a time warp did not enter my mind. Years later I did wonder about the possibility of a time warp but even then was not sure what one of these things was.

'The possibility of a mistake on my part never entered my mind, at thirteen train spotting was a very serious business and we were all eagle-eyed and mistakes did not happen.

'Over the years I thought from time to time about those mysterious happenings, the memory is still very clear in my mind and although I have been over and over it in my mind the facts remain completely unsolved.

'One thing is certain, what were two trains doing running so close together? That alone is a complete mystery.'

36

THE TRAIN IN THE NIGHT!

The village of West Dereham lies on a branch line that served four villages, Denver, Ryston, Abbey and West Dereham and the terminus at Stoke Ferry. The Great Northern line that runs south from King's Lynn to Ely and the branch line was situated almost half way between the two towns. Passenger traffic was withdrawn on 22 September, 1930 and final closure to goods and the cessation of railway services took place on 31 January 1966.

The feature of our story, West Dereham, was formerly known as Abbey, then was West Dereham on 1 January 1886. The name was changed again on 1 July 1923 to Abbey and West Dereham and that is how it stayed until the closure of the station.

Mr A. Dixon of West Bridgeford near Nottingham writes to tell me of a very strange occurrence that happened to him and his wife whilst they were living in West Dereham in 1954–5.

Mr Dixon worked on a local farm on the outskirts of the village, which in those days only had the benefit of a goods service, which I suspect only ran when demand warranted it. The farmers used it to convey their produce, and general goods were carried on occasions.

One night Mr Dixon woke with a start, he could hear a noise; he leapt out of bed and peered out of the window. The Dixons' house commanded a view over the railway where it ran through the village. Mrs Dixon, waking up, wanted to know what the excitement was about. She soon joined her husband at the window; they both listened, they could hear the sound of a train coming to the village, the clear night seemed to amplify the unmistakable sound of a steam engine getting nearer. They looked at each other, then peered out of the window again, then they saw it – an engine pulling two coaches passing slowly along the rusting line. As it slowly chuffed out of sight the Dixons were puzzled, where would a passenger train be running to at around 3am, who would be opening the gates and operating the signals? Still wondering they returned to bed and sleep.

The following day Mr Dixon mentioned the incident to his workmates on the farm. They looked at each other and grinned, one man said 'You've been dreaming, no passenger train has run down this line for years.' But the Dixons were adamant, they knew what they had seen and it was very real to them and neither could be accused of romancing or being under the influence of drink.

Mr and Mrs Dixon went to have a look at the line; it was very rusty and overgrown and there was no sign of anything having travelled on it for a long time, although the goods did use it occasionally.

No solution has been offered to solve this incident and so it will remain an unanswered mystery.

37

A Stranger In The Fog

This story is one that is timeless and it loses nothing for repeating. Its drama is retained and although it goes back to 1917 it could have happened many years later.

Henry Kirkup didn't believe in ghosts, he was a contented man, fond of his pint of beer and a bet on the horses, but one thing was absolutely certain, he was level-headed and had no time for ghosts. If anyone of his acquaintances admitted to having seen a spook Henry would laugh him out of the room.

However, after his experience with a ghost Henry was a changed man and no longer laughed at tales of the supernatural.

One winter's evening in 1917, Henry, a sergeant in a northern regiment, was hurrying down Westgate Road in Newcastle where he owned a trim little home. He was groping his way through a particularly thick, acrid fog which had descended like a blanket over the area. Henry was making for Newcastle Central Station and he had nearly lost his bearings when a voice came to him out of the gloom. 'Are you lost, mate?' Henry gasped in surprise. 'I want to go to Central Station,' he replied. 'That's all right,' replied the voice, 'I'm going there myself, keep close and we'll get there somehow.' Henry gratefully fell in beside the stranger who had now emerged out of the fog.

Westgate Road was very quiet, the muffled sounds from the industrial premises seemed strangely muted, the air was damp and cold, it penetrated the clothing. The fog was acrid and made talking somewhat painful so the two men didn't try to converse. As they passed through pools of light carved into the fog by the hissing gas lamps Henry Kirkup took a glance at his companion who was now revealed by his flashes to be a sergeant in a southern regiment. Henry noticed, however, that the soldier's uniform was of a kind worn in the South African War some sixteen years earlier. Henry was just going to ask the other why he was wearing such an outdated old uniform when the stranger spoke. 'Are you going back to your unit?' Henry said he was.

'So am I,' said the other, 'I have to catch a train from here to London.'

'I too,' said Henry. 'We could travel together, for company of course.'

'Sure,' replied the other, 'I'll be pleased to have some-one to talk to.'

On arrival at Newcastle Central Station they found the train waiting, they soon found an empty compart-ment. By this time the fog was beginning to clear and Henry could see one or two stars glowing faintly in the winter sky.

'This night is similar to one night in 1899. I will never forget it,' the stranger remarked.

Henry was interested, 'A long time to remember 1899!'

'I have very good reason to remember it' said the South African sergeant. He blew his nose, 'I'll tell you about it. I was pleased with myself that night. I had found an empty compartment and I settled down to doze a little; then a man got in, and sat down opposite me looking at me in a shifty way, he looked mean, and ill at ease, but I was tired, I'd done a hard day's work recruiting for the regiment in Newcastle. I felt in my pocket for a cigarette and I accidentally pulled out my wallet and my pay packet which spilled out onto the floor. I picked it all up but the other man was watching me intently like a dog watches a rabbit. I was almost dropping off to sleep with fatigue when the man leapt up and made a lunge at me, he had a long knife. I grabbed his wrist and deflected the blade of the knife whereupon we both

96

rolled about on the floor.' Henry asked, 'Did you win the fight?'

'No,' said the stranger. 'Although my attacker was very thin he was stronger than me and as I tried to reach the window communicating cord he pulled me back and plunged the knife into my chest.'

'But were you lucky? Did you deflect the blade into a less vulnerable spot?' asked Henry feeling slightly sick at the gruesome description of the fight.

'No,' said the other, 'I was unlucky, he did not miss, he killed me.'

'He did what?' gasped Henry, looking across the compartment. He couldn't believe his eyes, the stranger had gone, dissolved into thin air. Henry was on his own in the compartment as the train drew further and further away from Newcastle.

38

THE VISITOR

I cannot think of a more bizarre situation than when one goes into a platelayer's hut to have a snack and sit quite comfortably munching away when a ghost walks in and goes to the far corner and stands gazing into the dark recesses. Such is the experience of my correspondent Mr C. Whitehead, who kindly sent me his memories of the startling event.

The story begins in the late 1950s when Mr Whitehead was employed by British Railways as a platelayer on the main line between Ramsbottom and Helmshore. This was before Dr Beeching wielded his axe with such malignant venom on the railways of Great Britain. The line was losing money, mainly due, I suspect, to the diversion of passenger traffic to make a case for closure.

Shortly before Mr Whitehead arrived to take his part in the maintenance of the line, two members of the gang were having a go at each other, niggling at first, but feelings were strained between these two men and matters were getting worse.

Then one day the two men were nearly at one anothers' throats and it took the others in the gang to keep them apart. One of the gang was walking the length, looking at the condition of the track, checking the fishplates, possible broken rails, and pumping ballast, when he came across a platelayers' cabin with the door open; fearing the cabin had been broken into and the tools stolen he ventured inside. He had hardly got inside the building when he was killed by a vicious blow from an axe wielded by one of the quarrelling men who had killed the wrong man! From then on the cabin was known as 'The Murder Cabin'.

It was some time later when Mr Whitehead came across the spectre of the murdered man who had made his presence known to several permanent way workers; they had nicknamed him 'George'.

Mr Whitehead was walking his length, the weather had been threatening rain and when the heavens opened, Mr Whitehead had to run for cover. Seeing the cabin nearby he raced to it and sought shelter; it was dark in the small building but it was dry and it served a purpose. He hadn't been there long when a shadow fell across the door, a man walked in and went over to the far corner and stood silently. Mr Whitehead shivered, it had suddenly turned quite cold. The rain was still coming down fast, the stranger didn't move, and Mr Whitehead didn't seem very menaced by the other presence so he sat still and waited for the rain to stop.

Eventually the rain stopped and the sun came out, Mr Whitehead got up and walked out into the fresh air. The stranger followed him and disappeared into the air like a puff of smoke, our friend couldn't believe his eyes. Some weeks later the whole gang were crushed into one of these cabins to shelter from the elements. The air was thick with smoke and the earthy smell of human beings crushed together. The door opened and 'George' walked in, he glided through the men to the far corner and stood in his usual posture gazing into the darkness. Mr Whitehead then told the foreman of his experience of meeting George in the old cabin. The foreman didn't laugh or pour scorn on Mr Whitehead's revelation, he just said, 'Don't worry, he won't hurt you, he often comes in to see us.'

I understand his murderer was caught and paid the ultimate penalty for this dreadful crime.

Today the track and other infrastructure has been removed between Ramsbottom and Helmshore and so too have the old platelayers' cabins. I wonder if 'George' still wanders about looking for the cabins that he used to frequent in search of his old workmates . . .

39

GHOSTS AT KIDLINGTON

On Christmas Eve 1874, a train packed with people returning home for the seasonal festivities was derailed when an axle broke on one of the carriages near Shipton-on-Cherwell. Eight carriages left the track and plunged down a steep embankment between the bridges over the River Cherwell. Thirty-four people died in the resultant fire and crash, and over a hundred were injured.

Now a remarkable series of events have happened in a modern terraced house at the Moor, Kidlington, less than a mile from the scene of the tragedy. Ask Mr Brian Beck if he believes in ghosts. Mr Beck lives at the Moor which is the terraced house I have mentioned – and Mr Beck will answer 'I haven't any choice, have I?. It isn't imagination when you're lying in bed and you suddenly see the figure of a child move across the room and disappear through a closed door.'

Many other things happen too in the Beck household; babies are heard crying, a poltergeist is very active moving things all over, lights go on and off, doors open and shut on their own, sounds of footsteps are heard all over the house.

At a Tupperware Party held in the house, several ladies were astonished when scratching and tapping noises were heard to come from a glass-topped coffee table. One lady had to be taken home in a very distressed state swearing that she would never enter the house again.

Mr Beck has been visited by the ghost of a lady who materialises in solid form, no haze no mist but absolutely life-like. Her visits are nocturnal and she arrives through the closed door and approaches the bed; on one occasion

Mr Beck awoke to find this lady, dressed in black and with a very sorrowful face, peering at him. Again when Mr Beck was reading in bed one night the lady appeared and put the light out. Mr Beck describes her as under forty, dressed in black, her hair done up in a bun, or tied neatly back under her bonnet; she seemed to be around for possibly thirty seconds to one minute. Mr Beck didn't feel very scared, more curious to find out her identity; she disappeared as mysteriously as she arrived.

Mrs Beck described an incident concerning her son Kye, only two and a half years old at the time, and certainly not able to use a pen. He surprised his parents by drawing a star of David in a neat and steady hand. He often said to his mother, 'I can't get to sleep, please tell the children to leave the toys alone.'

A neighbour has gone on record as seeing a woman and two children, followed by a man, walking towards the house, up the garden path then just disappearing . . . 'Cold' spots are noted in the house; one peculiar event was the morning Mrs Beck came down to find the gas cooker 'sparkling clean'; one spot near the bathroom has a strong smell of ripe apples, other smells in the house are of burning ashes and cooking, but not of this world!

How do we relate this bizarre litany of events with the horror of the train crash?

Some of the victims of the accident were taken to Hampton Gay Paper Mill to await identification; an artist from *The London Illustrated News*, in an issue dated January 1875, described the appalling scene.

> One instance, I witnessed, of heart-rending grief will remain indelibly imposed on my mind. Among the dead lay a young and handsome youth of about twenty-one awaiting identification. Hearing the rustle of a lady's dress close by my attention was fixed on the lady who had just entered. She was anxiously scanning the many bodies and in a moment singled out the handsome features of the dead boy. She fell prostrate with grief over the cold, white face of her son, raining kisses on his lips that could never return her love.

Beside her was the father sobbing uncontrollably, silently watched by a policeman.

How does the drawing of the woman made by the artist shortly after the accident compare with Mr Beck's nocturnal visitor? Mr Beck says there is a striking resemblance and the expression on her face is always the same; but why does she always come to this house when the crash happened nearly a mile away all those years ago?

With the coaches catching fire as of course they would, as they were wooden and were lit by gas, that would account for the strong smell of burning ashes experienced by the Becks. Mr and Mrs Beck have, however, decided to continue to live with the phenomena and do not intend to move.

A family who lived in the Beck's house previously also heard strange noises and heavy distinct footsteps in a bedroom. They didn't stay . . .

It would seem that the paranormal events are tied in closely with the train crash and the lady in black is still looking for her son. Is it possible that some of the victims might have been taken to a building on the site of Mr Beck's house?

One must admire the courage and resilience of the Becks who will not allow a supernatural force to drive them out of their house.

40
GAS LAMPS AND GHOSTS?

It was a dark night in November 1981, I was the crossing keeper at Damens Station and was waiting for the passage of the last down train from Keighley. The station stood empty, a light covering of frost lay illuminated by the incandescent glow from the gas lamps on the platform. Inside the signal box, the gas lights were also lit and the fire in the pot-bellied stove was glowing red hot.

I looked across at the empty station house, there was no one stopping there tonight. It was often empty now, Annie had left after her husband Norman died last Christmas; the nearest life was the main Halifax road about half a mile up the hill, what a lonely outpost!

At least I had already brought in the lamp from the up home signal. I had just to see the last train up the hill, then lock the gates, bring in the gate lamps and the down home lamp, lock up the signal box then go home.

Where was the train? It should have left Keighley five minutes ago. The clock ticked away, ever so slowly, it seemed. From my couch I glanced up the line towards the loop, I couldn't see the loop box from the cutting, just the rods of the loop's down starter signals, and my own reflection in the glass, but what was the shadow behind me looking into the box? I froze; at least the door was bolted, the shadowy figure moved off down the platform, or so it seemed from the reflection. I pulled myself together and dashed out of the door . . . 'Who's there?' expecting to hear one of the local gypsy lads running off. But not a sound. A shiver shot down my back, I lit a cigarette and went back into the box, bolted the door and sat down again, where was that train?

I looked up the line again, all I saw was my reflection, and then that shadowy figure again, it was clearer this time and appeared to be wearing some sort of railway uniform. It certainly had a peaked cap but no visible face!

I spun round and dashed outside straight away; not a sound, no one was there, just an uncanny silence. The river was silent as was the little stream at the end of the platform, even the normally busy main road was quiet now. What was that? A loud shriek told me that the Midland 4F had whistled for the foot crossing, the train was here at last. The staff at Keighley must have been eager to get home as they hadn't phoned. I darted to the crossing and opened the gates, getting the down home signal pulled off just in time. The train stormed through the tiny station unaware of the goings on there, I belled the train on to the next station. I closed the crossing gates and was up and down the signal like a cat after a bird. I pulled the shutters down, turned the gas off, locked the door and dashed off home.

I mused, were the gas lamps playing tricks? Or one of the gypsies, or was it really a ghost? What ever it was I have taken steps to make sure that I have not been there alone at night from that day to this!

41

THE MAN IN THE MIST

If one is to believe statistics, only two per cent of the world's population are gifted with 'second sight' or the ability to witness paranormal phenomena, but how many of these fortunate or unfortunate people ever realise this power? It will happen to them maybe once in a lifetime, often with horrific memories of their experiences. The following story is an example of an incident that left an indelible mark in my correspondent's memory.

Mr Alistair Robertson was returning to his home in Edinburgh after a business trip to London. On arriving at King's Cross he found a seat in the 'open plan' coach, put his case on the luggage rack and settled himself down for a good read. The coach was quite full with the usual business executives chatting away. Alistair had made the journey many times and thought he knew every mile of the journey intimately. He had bought a paperback at the W. H. Smith bookstall at King's Cross; it was a war story and certainly nothing to do with the supernatural so after reading the daily paper he started to read his new book. At this stage I must inform the reader that Alistair Robertson did not tell anyone of his horrific experience for many years, the incident being so incredible and beyond belief.

The coach he was in was alive with the usual hum of conversation and noise, not offensive but somewhat soporific and he began to nod off. He felt himself falling asleep and shook himself to shake the fatigue out of his system, he opened the ventilator and the breeze was most refreshing. The clickety-click of the rail joints seemed louder and made a reassuring sound and after a while he closed the ventilator and read some more of his book.

After about one and a half hours the train entered a tunnel and it turned out to be a very long tunnel; but the story had only just begun . . . Alistair was reading his book and was somewhat annoyed when the usual carriage lights didn't come on, so he put his book down and waited for daylight to return.

But then a very strange occurrence happened, he was suddenly aware of what appeared to be a form of mist forming over the seat opposite him, this puzzled Alistair as it was absolutely pitch black in the carriage. He thought at first that it must be steam drifting in from the steam heating system but he lifted his hand to his face to find he couldn't see it. He looked at the mist again and it began to swirl about but still over the table in front of him and the seat opposite.

Alistair was becoming mesmerised by the strange experience; the mist was gradually resolving itself into the shape of an oldish man, nearly bald but well dressed in a well-cut city suit, the picture was somewhat redolent of a bank manager or some other business executive, definitely respectable. He was a happy man seemingly because he was smiling; by his face he was about fifty-five years old, fairly plump, but everything about him seemed absolutely normal. It was just the way he had appeared that was so dramatic, he had a fuzz around him that remained to tantalise and Alistair wanted to be reassured of his normality.

This mist continued to swirl about him, mesmerising Alistair who was wide eyed with surprise.

The man just sat and smiled at Alistair who was covered in confusion. Alistair noticed that amid the swirling mist behind the newcomer there appeared to be a window and through it he could see a kind of crowd of people all milling about. They appeared to be moaning and wailing as if in great distress.

The man still smiled at Alistair, putting his hands on the table that separated them and leaning towards him. The fixed smile now became rather sinister, and began to assume grotesque proportions, he seemed to be rising out of the seat coming closer and closer to Alistair, who was now terrified and was trying to force himself back into his seat. The man's leering face was moving closer to the other face, there seemed nothing to stop it, this nightmare . . .

Alistair then thought about the other people in the carriage who were so close but so far away; the puzzling thing was that he couldn't see them or even hear them and this discovery didn't exactly help his sinking courage. As the man grew closer, Alistair could even feel the man's breath or thought he could.

Summoning up the remains of his courage Alistair thrust his hand outwards at the face to ward it off, but to his surprise he never touched anything, the man leaned back and continued to smile but again the 'smile' had become a sinister leer, menacing . . .

Then to Alistair's relief the mist's swirl was gradually dissipating, reducing the man's shape to a vague outline. Alistair shook himself, bewildered by the whole sequence of events Eventually the mist cleared completely and the man and the crowd of people behind him disappeared, the sounds of conversation of his fellow travellers returned, the sound of the rail joints were there, normality was supreme.

Alistair stood up and stretched, yawned, and looked out of the window, the passing countryside seemed so reassuring. He puzzled and gazed at the empty seat opposite, there was nothing to be seen at all. The two men sitting across the gangway were chatting happily, all seemed normal, but who was the man? And why did he appear? These questions are still unanswered and perhaps always will be . . .

42
THE MAN
IN THE BLACK BERET

This story concerns a young man who, one cold December afternoon, was incredibly caught up in a time warp that baffles him to this day. He witnessed a replay of an accident in which a man was run over by a steam locomotive. Our young man was both horrified and helpless as he saw in graphic detail this appalling accident.

Our tale begins in a very innocuous way. Young Andy had just left school and at the time of the incident, set in the 1960s, he was able to find a job with British Railways as an apprentice signalman. However, his first duties saw him very actively engaged in the removal of redundant signalling equipment, eg signals, signal boxes, etc, as part of the updating and modernisation of post-war British Railways.

Andy was working with two mates, Alf and Ron, who were older and much more experienced in the world of signalling expertise; these two men were to instruct Andy in the initial part of his training. This particular day was quite bright for December and the three men enjoyed the ten-mile journey to the local village where they had to dismantle the redundant signal cabin. The senior man, Alf, detailed Andy to remove the levers from the frame and load them into the BR van.

About 3pm Alf asked Andy if he would walk to the nearby village and get them some cigarettes and chocolate as the men wanted a break.

Andy set off for the village along the deserted track which was by now rusting. One could see the rusted track through the over-powering spread of weeds and other undergrowth. He reached the village, purchased the cigarettes and chocolate, looked round the village then started to walk back munching a bar of chocolate. He reached the old railway line and continued on his way back, this time walking on the sleepers. It was beginning to get dusk and the clouds were hastening the end of a winter's day.

He was about halfway back when he heard a noise that made his hair stand on end, the noise of a steam engine – was it possible? He looked around, nothing in sight, then faintly on the slight breeze he heard it again, the unmistakable sound of a steam engine and it was approaching. Andy knew that steam motive power had ceased in this area many years ago; anyway the line had been closed to all traffic for months so what was such an engine doing on the line now? He quickened his pace, he knew something was wrong and now felt as if he wanted to get as far away from the place as possible. Panic set in when the sound of the engine appeared much louder, he stumbled on the sleepers and fell face down. He could hear the loco as if it was almost upon him, he turned to look and an amazing sequence of events evolved before his eyes. The whole area was a haze of yellow light that seemed somehow menacing, he tried to get to his feet but for some reason couldn't, then he heard the blood-curdling sound of the shriek of an engine's whistle! It split the December air with its piercing note.

Then Andy saw the tall figure of a man dressed in railway uniform and wearing a black beret instead of the regulation railway hat; Andy thought the beret was like those worn by the Royal Tank Corps. The figure stood in the track seemingly rooted to the spot and made no move to avoid the oncoming engine. There was a horrible piercing scream from the figure as the engine struck it and ground it into pulp under the engine.

At last Andy found his feet and ran as fast as he

could back to the other men; he leapt through the door and collapsed in a heap on the floor.

When Alf had revived him with a cup of strong tea he poured out his story. 'Don't be daft,' they scoffed. 'I tell you I saw him killed,' gasped Andy, 'and he was wearing a black beret like the Tank Corps wear.' Alf stroked his chin, 'A black beret'. Then the recollections came flooding back to the two older men and Alf then told Andy the story. 'I remember now, about nine or ten years ago there was a bloke killed doing track maintenance work around here, he wore a black beret and was well known. I think he had been in the Tank Corps or something like that, but you wouldn't know anything about that would you?' Andy replied that it was a bit before his time and they all laughed.

Without further ado the three men loaded the van and drove back to Darlington and vowed never to return to the area again; another gang finished the job. No further sign was seen of the phantom engine or if it was ever seen again nobody ever admitted it.

Andy is now happily married with two fine children and when they ask about ghosts Andy shakes his head.

43
THE REVENGE
OF THE OLD SOLDIER

The type of supernatural phenomenon that returns to wreak revenge for an earthly feud is fortunately in the minority, but ghosts that kill are still evident in certain circumstances.

Tom Howe was an engine driver, he was also a highly skilled engineer and in his youth had been apprenticed to a firm of railway engineers at Doncaster. He was a burly, well-built man, liked by his workmates, he had a practical disposition and he certainly didn't believe in ghosts or the occult.

In 1901 Tom moved from the North to London and he set up a family home for his wife and daughter near King's Cross Station. Later that year he met an old friend, Len Curtis, with whom he had worked at Doncaster. Curtis had moved to London earlier so it was a happy reunion when their acquaintance was renewed. Eventually Howe became fireman to Curtis on the midnight expresses to the northern capital.

When World War I began the two men served together in the 42nd Division at Gallipoli. Later, again they were to work together in the same link. Len Curtis married and Howe was his best man at the nuptials. Unknown to both men this is just where the trouble that was to end their friendship began – it would appear that the two families became very friendly and visited each others' homes regularly. However, Howe became very fond of Ellen Curtis and was taken with her charm and companionship especially as Ellen was fifteen years younger than her husband.

Tom Howe eventually became a driver and often his route would take him past the Curtis home at Finsbury Park; whenever Howe had any spare time he would visit Ellen, telling his own wife that he had business elsewhere. Eventually Ellen Curtis had a baby and the local rumours at Finsbury Park whispered that Howe was the father.

Then news of Howe's interest in his wife reached Len Curtis who was beside himself with fury; when he met Howe again he pulled Howe out of the cab of a loco and threatened him not to see his wife again.

The next day Howe was transferred to the early morning express to Newcastle via York; even so the train was on the same line that ran past the Curtis home and unknown to her husband Ellen used to wave to Howe as he passed on his regular run and on the homeward run she would wave an oil lamp.

One wet Saturday night Howe noticed from the cab of his Atlantic that Ellen's signal lamp was for the first time missing; he slowed down for the network of points near the Curtis home and whistled up but there was no sign of Ellen. As he cycled home from the shed he noticed the newsbill of the local paper, 'TRAGEDY IN RAILWAY COTTAGE, ENGINE DRIVER KILLS HIS WIFE AND CHILD THEN COMMITS SUICIDE.'

The following day Tom Howe found out that his former workmate and friend had murdered his family and then killed himself.

Time passed by with its usual routine. Howe always looked out of the cab when he reduced speed for the points and glanced at the old cottage where the Curtis family had lived, more out of habit than morbid curiosity. One night a horrific series of events occurred that was to cost Howe his life.

Tom Howe as usual moved the regulator to slow down for the points near the Curtis abode; he leaned out of the cab as usual to look for the cottage when his fireman yelled at him with a terrified look on his face.

The fireman pointed to the regulator that was moving on its own into the open position. The train was now gathering speed approaching the points and Howe to his horror saw the wraith of Curtis holding the regulator wide open, but the strange thing was that Curtis was wearing the uniform of the 42nd Division, the one he had worn at Gallipoli!

Howe made a grab for the regulator to pull it back to reduce speed, but the lever was solid, no movement. Howe saw the ghostly figure disappear into the steam, the engine, by now completely out of control, hit the points at this crazy speed, derailed and hit the embankment wall. Howe was killed instantly but the fireman survived to vow that the ghost of Len Curtis had returned to wreak a terrible revenge.

44

THE VICTORIAN
RAILWAY DISASTER

Nineteen-year-old Pamela Goodsell's eyes nearly left their sockets when she saw what the light of a match revealed.

An old train, with the remains of passengers, now skeletal, lying in some disarray on the mouldering floor of the carriage. The train had been sealed up in an underground tunnel, but why?

Other remains of humans were lying all over the train; the unfortunate passengers were noticed to be wearing Victorian-style clothing, some of the men sported top hats. The teenager had fallen down a 20ft shaft while walking through the park near the site of the old Crystal Palace in south-east London.

Pamela was horrified by her discovery, yet of course very puzzled that the local authorities hadn't exhumed the remains and thus brought to light the fact of the mystery. Yet mystery there was because when she made enquiries about her find no one wanted to know. 'Completely preposterous', said London Transport. And they went on to say, 'There is no record of a subway train crash in the area.' However, that statement is certainly open to question.

The London Transport spokesman went on to say, 'We just don't lose trains and passengers like that, not even in Victorian times.'

Miss Goodsell, who said she had found the remains in 1978, could not find the shaft, however, when she went back to the park. But she remains quite unshakeable in her account of the horrific experience, and it seems that nearly all Sydenham knows that there is an abandoned underground train under the park somewhere, possibly the result of an experiment that went badly wrong, so it would appear that the story isn't all moonshine!

Legend has it that the train was shunted into a tunnel around 1870 and it was never seen again, or perhaps it was conveniently forgotten by the authorities who got the experiment badly wrong, preferring to bury their mistake for ever. One excuse put forward is that the relevant documents appertaining to the mystery were lost during the last war.

However, experts have been successful in tracing the mystery back to an experimental train designed by an engineer named T. W. Rammell, which once ran for 600 yards on a line between Sydenham Gate and Penge. Compressed air was pumped into the tunnel which had airtight doors and the train careered along at about 35mph . . . No record of any accident had been recorded, the experiment was soon discarded and no other prototype constructed; the train was evidently sealed up in its tunnel and forgotten by the outside world.

Now members of the London Underground Railway Society, I'm told, are showing a healthy interest, and I understand that they feel that they are near a breakthrough to crack this mystery once and for all.

The Norwood Historical Society also are interested and have combined with the former society to effect a solution. Then two societies have obtained permission to sink boreholes in the park to identify the site of the tunnel, special electronic tests have been made and are now being evaluated.

The chairman of the Norwood Historical Society has gone on record as saying that they are about to use more sophisticated electronic equipment and dig along the line of the old underground track.

The searchers are hoping to uncover the whole train intact and the outside world will be very interested to see what finds are evident. The people around the area cannot explain the occasional rumblings that are sometimes heard at different times of the year. Are they connected with this dreadful accident? Can they be explained?

45

THE WRECK
OF THE SCOTTISH MAIL

When driver Ben Fleetwood and fireman Jack Talbot reported for duty at two o'clock on the afternoon of 19 September 1906, they each had exactly nine hours left to live.

The manner of their dying was to leave behind what is probably the greatest unsolved mystery in British railway history.

Together they made a good, well-experienced, cheerful footplate crew. Fleetwood was a dignified, trusted, well-liked man of flawless character. Talbot was more than a fully competent, well-trained main line fireman. He was also a qualified driver and design engineer, and had been destined to be employed on the staff of the chief mechanical engineer.

If you were a passenger on a high-speed night express, here surely was a crew in which you could put your trust.

Their tour of duty for each day of this particular week was a straightforward little job of three separate trips.

After booking on at Doncaster sheds, they worked the three o'clock afternoon passenger train to York. From York they worked the 6.50 express to Peterborough, and from Peterborough they worked the London–Edinburgh night mail as far as Doncaster, where they were relieved and booked off duty.

This was a rostered job in the express passenger link and therefore came round to each footplate crew regularly every few weeks. Certainly Fleetwood and Talbot had worked this particular duty many times.

The engine was of a well-proven class and was virtually brand new – Jack Talbot, as part of his engineering apprenticeship, had helped to built it.

Both men knew the route thoroughly, the locomotive was hauling a train well within its capabilities, the night was dry and fine, visibility was excellent, the train was running exactly to time and under clear green signals – yet this footplate crew and twelve of their unsuspecting passengers were about to die.

At a few minutes before eleven, the train was approaching Grantham, the only stop before Doncaster.

On the platform at Grantham stood a station inspector and a small group of post office employees. They were preparing for quick action, for they had a bare two minutes in which to haul almost a hundred mail bags into the mail vans of the train once it had stopped.

On this night it did not stop. The two signalmen and the small group on the platform looked on in petrified disbelief and horror as the night mail thundered headlong into the station.

Wreathed in steam, and bathed in the crimson glow from the open firebox, the locomotive lurched along the platform in a volcanic nightmare of sound and fury. It passed safely through the station, disappeared out into the darkness at the north end of the station – then left the rails.

It was a crash of appalling destruction, a holocaust of mangled timber and metal which soon became a funeral pyre. The crackle of the flames, the hiss of escaping steam, the shouts of arriving rescuers, the screams of the dying, became a horrifying amalgam of tragic sound that stunned the senses of those further people running up to help.

The locomotive was completely and utterly wrecked. Daylight revealed it as a mangled, tangled heap of twisted steel which could give no clue to the cause of the disaster. Neither could Fleetwood or Talbot. They had been killed instantly.

The investigation – for all the light it threw on the matter – might as well never have been held.

This was no fault of the investigators. There was literally nothing to investigate, no objects to examine, no person to question and no papers to read.

The night mail had stormed at high speed through Grantham Station, raced out into the darkness – and crashed.

The stark simplicity of that statement says all that can really be said about this mystery. Various people offered a miscellany of improbable solutions, but no one explanation held much more water than any other.

If there was a popular theory, it was simply that both men had forgotten where they were on the railway line in relation to Peterborough and Grantham. But Grantham was a busy, well lit station and the two signal gantries guarding it from the south had a signal layout which was totally unique to Grantham. Either man on the footplate could read this signal layout as easily as telling the time by the town hall clock.

It was easily proved that they were both awake. The signalmen had a clear view of the footplate and both enginemen were standing on their respective sides of the footplate, the driver at the controls and the fireman standing close to the boiler front, as the train came storming into Grantham Station.

So the wreck of the Scottish mail passed into railway legend and whatever happened on the footplate of the locomotive that tragic, horrifying night – none of us shall ever know.

46

THE HEXTHORPE GHOST

My story takes place one dark night in late autumn at the Cherry Tree sidings at Hexthorpe one mile west of Doncaster. The sidings were in those days used mainly for coal and coal empties traffic, and it was while shunting empty coal wagons that the following incident took place.

My second man and myself were looking through the rear windows of our diesel locomotive awaiting a signal from the yard staff. After a minute or so the shunter signalled us with his lamp to proceed down the yard to attach a rake of wagons. As I turned to open the power controller on the loco I noticed the figure of a man coming across the adjoining tracks towards us. He appeared to be dressed in a light coloured mackintosh and cap. I lowered the cab window and shouted, 'Hey, where do you think you're going?.' He ignored my question and by now had reached the line on which we stood. Although I could clearly see his outline and had no doubt whatsoever that it was a man, I could not see his face or features, only his cap and a dark mask where his face would normally be. By now he had passed out of my sight at the rear of the loco. Turning to my second man I said, 'Has that bloke come out clear on your side?' 'No there's no one here,' he replied. At the same time we both climbed down the steps at either side of the loco and met at the rear centre. The man was nowhere to be seen. By now the shunter had walked up the siding to where we stood and asked what was wrong. I told him what had happened, the three of us again searched all around the loco and surrounding sidings, but to no avail. There was no sign of anyone. The shunter said that he had heard of the ghost of a man sitting on the buffer stops at the end of the sidings but thought that his mates were trying to frighten him. Now he wasn't so sure.

Two weeks later I was in the signal box at St James Junction which is at the opposite end of Hexthorpe yard to where the above sighting took place. I was waiting to conduct a Tinsley train crew into the Decoy marshalling yard at Doncaster. During my conversation with the signalman I mentioned the ghost. He was very startled and uneasy for a minute or so and then went on to tell me of what had happened the last time he had been on nights in that box.

He had a train of wagons bound for Wath-on-Dearne, stood in his section and the brake van was about twenty yards beyond the signal box. All was quiet when all of a sudden he heard someone shouting. Before he could get to the door of the box it burst open and in staggered a guard. According to the signalman the poor fellow was in such a state that he could neither stand nor speak. 'I sat him down and quickly made him a cup of tea,' said the signalman. After a while the guard who was in charge of the train outside the signal box was able to tell what had happened. He had been sitting quietly in his brake van waiting for the train to move off when the rear door of the van opened and a man in a light rain coat had walked in and without saying a word had gone out of the other door without opening it. In other words he had walked through a closed door. It is obvious that this was the same ghost as the one I had seen two weeks earlier. Who he was or why he was there I don't know to this day, but I do know that he *was* there and maybe still is.

47
THE LETTER

'Goodbye son,' said Mrs Ayscough, who tried hard not to weep but yielded to nature and brushed the tear away with her glove. 'Goodbye mother . . . and don't worry. We shall all be home by Christmas. They've got the Kaiser on the run already. I doubt if they'll even need us.'

But his last words were drowned in a hiss of escaping steam and Mrs Ayscough waved and waved until not only the train had vanished from view but until everyone had left the platform.

'There, there, Mrs Ayscough . . .' It was Tom Farrow the station master. 'Don't take on so. Your Bob'll be home before you know where you are.'

He put his arm gently round her shoulder and guided her to the station entrance. She went reluctantly and he watched her set off for her house down Station Road.

That night Mrs Ayscough said her prayers. She always said her prayers but that night she said her prayers more fervently than usual. She tried to imagine Bob far away in France, translating him in her mind to a foreign field. But the field she conjured up bore a marked resemblance to the field next door to her house where Bob had played in his childhood.

She thought about her son every day, prayed for him every evening and looked forward to the first letter he had promised to write to her.

But when the letter came it was not brought by the postman. Mr Farrow the station master brought it. It was a small letter, a letter in a brown envelope, an envelope without a stamp and with OHMS written upon it.

Mr Farrow stayed with her until she had read the

letter's brief sentence and he stayed with her until the light faded and until she went to bed, alone, to pray and to merciful sleep.

The following day Mrs Ayscough walked down the road to the railway station. She thanked Mr Farrow for his kindness and stood on the platform, gazing down the line, listening to the wind in the telegraph wires, looking at the silver ribbons of rail as they converged and curved away into the cutting beyond the village.

She came again the next day and Mr Farrow watched from his office window as Mrs Ayscough stood alone, keeping a solitary vigil, staring into the distance.

She did it every day. And when, in November 1918, the war came to an end, she still did it. She walked to the station in all weathers, always alone, always at the same time and stood for about five minutes transfixed.

In 1958 at the age of eighty Mrs Ayscough died. Two years later the village railway line was closed.

For some time the railway station stood empty and deserted. The signals and the signboards were all removed and, one day, the premises were bought and converted into a house.

Maureen and John Parker made an excellent job of the alterations and lived happily at Station House for many years.

As newcomers they knew nothing of either Mr Farrow or of Mrs Ayscough or of Mrs Ayscough's only son . . . until one night after Christmas in 1981.

It had been a bitterly cold day and that night a blizzard sprang up. The Parkers, snug indoors, were about to go to bed when, simultaneously they both felt they heard shouting outside.

The noise of the storm was by this time so great that both doubted their own ears. But someone seemed to be calling 'Bob' and another voice seemed to reply 'Mother'.

They stood still in the hall at the foot of the stairs,

listening, craning, and John Parker stepped to the window and drew back the curtains.

Looking out across the platform he thought he could discern the figure of an old lady, standing by the platform edge staring up what had been the railway track.

And when he looked again there was another figure moving towards her, a man, a soldier . . . in a peaked cap and carrying a slung rifle.

Parker motioned his wife to join him but when he looked back there was no one there. There was no woman, no soldier, only drifting snow, driving and piling up outside the door.

Despite his wife's protests that he was on a fool's errand Parker struggled into his coat and boots and strode out into the blizzard and along the edge of the platform.

There was not a soul in sight nor were there voices nor footprints in the snow nor any living mortal thing.

He returned to the house, closed the door behind him, took off his coat shedding snow on the carpet. It was only when he took off his boots that he noticed the piece of brown paper sticking to the sole.

Carefully he removed it and, brushing the snow from it, saw that it was an envelope, a small brown envelope, an envelope with the initials OHMS stamped upon it.

And there was a letter in it, a letter just one line long, a line that began: 'Dear Mrs Ayscough, I regret to inform you . . .'

48

THE STRANGE HAPPENINGS
AT SHARPTHORNE TUNNEL

The mysteries of the paranormal will always be complex and will assume many different types of phenomena.

I have visited many disused railway stations and have walked miles of former trackbed without experiencing any feelings other than sadness and inveterate loss of a form of travel. So far I have yet to experience a ghostly sound or sighting but perhaps I am unlucky! Sometimes I wish that I could have the sense of being able to lift the veil like so many of my kind correspondents, but they tell me that I am lucky.

To some people, the ability to participate in a paranormal event seems so easy it appears as if these people generate and possibly energise the sequence of events that result in a phenomenon. Take the story of a friend of mine; a level-headed, no-nonsense disbeliever who had a traumatic experience in a disused tunnel in the south of England.

During the early 1960s, my friend was spending some time around the Bluebell Line in rural, leafy Sussex when he decided to go and have a look at the sad removal of track and facilities at West Hoathly. This station is situated north-west of Horsted Keynes which is the northern terminal of the Bluebell Line; and Sharpthorne Tunnel is situated on the line from Lewes to East Grinstead. It was a Saturday and the workmen were having their weekend off, so the place was deserted. The old station was a sad sight without any commuters to give it life. It stood empty, abandoned, left to rot until some unfeeling demolition firm would raze it to the ground; removing a way of life.

Everything was quiet and the autumn leaves were

covering the ground; the now lifeless trackbed telling its own story. After examining the station my friend decided to walk down the trackbed to find the tunnel which he had heard about. He walked into the cutting and saw the mouth of the tunnel ahead; it was a very straight tunnel and he could see the bright sunlight at the end of the bore. He decided to go in and explore; the track had been removed but the entrances hadn't been sealed yet. Consulting his notes, he discovered that the tunnel was nearly half a mile long. He ventured in, the sound of his footfalls on the still existent ballast was somewhat reassuring; he was conscious of the darkness as he progressed further into the tunnel.

Now and again, he paused and looked back to the receding sight of the old station; then he looked ahead to the welcoming arc of sunlight at the other end of the tunnel; the sound of water dripping from the vaulted brick roof was rhythmic and evocative.

He had been progressing steadily for perhaps ten minutes when suddenly he became aware of another presence in the tunnel. He stopped and listened; only the constant drip of water, sometimes near at hand, sometimes distant, broke the silence.

Then my friend's hair rose on the back of his neck as a figure flitted from one side of the tunnel to the other. Passing the bright arc of sunlight, it was unmistakable; it happened; he saw it. It made no sound, which was strange as the ballast had echoed my friend's footsteps. The figure was now lost in the shadows of the tunnel; was it hiding in a manhole? Or was it waiting in stealth to strike him? He stopped walking and peered into the stygian darkness. All manner of thoughts crowded his mind; what was the figure up to? Was it scavenging, or just some youth trying to frighten someone?

There was no sign of movement now and no light which was strange as anyone searching in the corners of this tunnel would need some sort of illumination. At this stage my friend hadn't thought of the supernatural; besides he didn't believe in that sort of thing . . . He looked back to the station end of the tunnel; it seemed a long way back. There was no sign of the figure, so he decided to go on a bit further, only to find that his legs would not move forward. He tried again; it was as if an invisible barrier was holding him back. He was really afraid now, and he decided to beat a dignified retreat. He turned and walked slowly back, his legs working perfectly. Just to assure himself, he again turned round and tried to go the other way. He was doing well when all of a sudden he came up against the invisible barrier again. He picked up a piece of ballast and threw it; he watched the stone disappear into the darkness then, 'boing', he ducked as he heard it hit something. It was no good, he would have to get out of the strange placed – once in the daylight, common sense would return.

It seemed a long way back to the cutting and station; he was sweating in his haste and he sat down on a low wall to think things out. He had been taking photographs before he entered the tunnel and he was certain that he hadn't seen anyone enter the tunnel, yet . . .

Admittedly he had only had a brief glimpse of the figure but it had made a lasting impression; he couldn't understand the events which seemed to have no logical explanation. Any other person in the tunnel at that time would have betrayed their presence by the sound of their footfalls on the thick ballast on the tunnel floor. As a matter of interest my friend has spoken to other people who have ventured into the depths of Sharpthorne Tunnel and they too have had a very strong feeling of being watched by something.

The paranormal seemed to have been at work; mystifying and tantalising the mortal that dared to venture into the darkness and damp gloom. Was the sinister figure a former casualty of some railway disaster who returns to the scene of the accident? So far no explanation has been offered.

ACKNOWLEDGEMENTS

I would like to thank the following people for supplying their stories: C. Barker, P. S. Chapman, B. J. Willey, J.J. Leslie, H. E. Caunt, C. E. Whitehead, H. C. Johnston, J. McIlmurray, J. Hallam, G. Leslie, R. J. Barry, P. Richardson, R. R. Mester, E. W. Poulter, Thorsons Publishing Group (Patrick Stephens Ltd), The Oxford Mail Newspaper Ltd, E. A. Shaw, R. J. Woodward, A. Dixon, M. A. Houghton, R. L. P. Belanger, P. Hussellbury, B. C. Essex, P. Craddock, D. M. Ross, J. Marshall, E. L. Anderson, D. Winn, M. Squires, A. Withnall, L. A. Whitehouse, P. Briggs, A. J. Ludlam, H. B. Brookes, B. Hamilton, C. Selway, I. McGill, P Screeton, and all other sources of help, direct and indirect, and the help and encouragement of my friends.